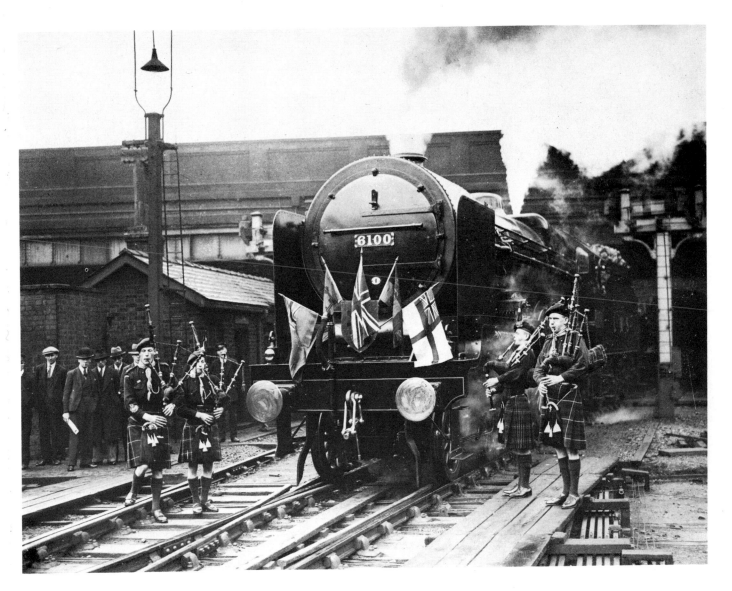

REFLECTIONS

A COLLECTION OF PHOTOGRAPHS FROM THE BBC HULTON PICTURE LIBRARY

BY

BOB ESSERY & NIGEL HARRIS

Silver Link Publishing Ltd

5 HAWK ST, CARNFORTH, LANCASHIRE, LA5 9LA

EUSTON

THE TWO principal constituents of the LMS were, without doubt, the London & North Western Railway and the Midland Railway whose respective London Termini were close to each other at Euston and St Pancras. The 'LNW' and MR had always been strong competitors and relations between the Companies had never been good, and in the early years of the LMS, it was the Midland which gained the upper hand — Midland livery was adopted for the locomotives, coaches and wagon stock. Midland locomotives became 'standard classes' and Midland operating methods became those of the newly-formed LMS, however the MR did not get its own way in everything and the newly formed Company, the largest joint stock company operating a transport system anywhere in the world, naturally chose to have its Headquarters at its principal London terminus — Euston, and so this seemed a good point at which to begin this look at the LMS.

It has already been stated, but it should be said again, that this book is not intended to be a history of the LMS. Nor is it meant to be a comprehensive pictorial record or illustrated survey. It is a look at the Company as recorded by the news photographers of the day who, being London-based tended to concentrate their efforts at the Southern end of the system. Fortunately they did spend a considerable amount of time in Euston which, regardless of what may be said elsewhere, was the most important railway terminus in the kingdom.

Supporters of other railways may advance their claims for an establishment a little to the East at Kings Cross, and perhaps they would suggest that the old Great Northern Station held a more important position in British Railway history. Claims would no doubt also come from those who saw

Above: The famous Doric Arch, photographed on August 11 1933. The posters on the right advertise the Dublin Horse Show which was being held on August 8–11 (and which featured Great International Military Jumping contests) and 'A Long Day Tour in the Wonderland of Wales', starting on Friday night August 8, departing from Euston at 1.00am. Return travel to Bangor cost 15/6, to Caernarvon 16/– and 17/3 to Llanberis. Regrettably the van behind the railings obstructs the rest of the wording but 'breakfasts and motor tours' also featured. The portico was built with Yorkshire stone from Bramley Fall Quarries and the largest stones weighed 13 tons. The total height of the portico was 72ft and the four Doric Columns were 44ft 2in high and 8ft 6in in diameter. The gilded word 'Euston' was not featured on the original design, and this was inscribed later, in 1870. In 1899 plans were made to extend Euston station south, towards the Euston Road but this plan was not carried through due to financial pressure on the Company at that time. In 1935 the LMS again announced plans to extend the station and the Company even went ahead to quarry 100,000 tons of limestone (see 'People & Special Events') but World War II prevented this scheme being completed and so it was left to British Railways to rebuild in the early 1960s, who removed for ever the Doric Arch and Hardwick's Great Hall.

Left: Photographed at Euston on August 25 1930, this picture shows the LMS information bureau, which was a new feature in the Great Hall at that time. Gazing down at the structure is the statue of George Stephenson, which is now preserved at the National Railway Museum.

Below: There was a difference of public opinion at the time as to whether this was the correct place in the station to locate an information Bureau but be that as it may, in 1930 an information and reservation office was established by the LMS in the Great Hall and this picture gives a clear view of the counter area, showing the facilities available for booking seats, making sleeper reservations and general inquiries.

Waterloo as being more important than Euston, after all it was larger, while without doubt, the followers of the Swindon tradition would suggest that further west at Paddington one could find the premier station in the land. But to all of these claims one would say that really it was Euston which was the 'Premier Station', a fitting title for the headquarters of the old LNWR, itself known as the 'Premier line' in the Kingdom at the time of the Grouping.

Before the British Railways rebuilding of the station in 1961/2 Euston occupied 18 acres, twice the size of neighbouring St Pancras, the Midland Railway's London terminus, according to the official LMS Handbook of Statistics, dated 1937. It was nevertheless still smaller than either Crewe or Manchester Victoria and Exchange (LYR/LNWR), the latter pair covering 23 acres each; they were separate stations, although joined together after the Grouping. Euston's 15 platform lines were exceeded only by Crewe with 16 and Manchester (Victoria & Exchange) with 21, but it was equalled by Birmingham New Street, Blackpool North and Preston (LNWR/LYR) all with 15 platform faces also. Euston's longest platform was 1,030ft. and the total length of its platforms was 10,776 feet:Its longest platform was shorter than the connecting platform at Manchester Victoria and Ex-

change, which at 2,194ft. was the longest platform in the kingdom and actually built by the LMS. Other stations which had platforms longer than those at Euston were at Carlisle (1,422ft.), Chester Joint (1,340ft.), Crewe (1,509ft.), Derby Midland (1,146ft.), Nottingham (1,177ft), Preston (1,253ft.), Rugby (1,415ft.), Sheffield Midland (1,313ft.), Southport Chapel Street (1,138ft.) and Willesden Main Line (1,210ft.). In Scotland, platforms at Aberdeen (1,596ft.) and Glas-

gow Central (1,040ft.) both exceeded Euston, while of course the old GSWR station at St Enoch, with a platform length of 1,128ft. had a longer face than any at Euston, but in addition St Enoch's 13½-acre area made it the largest of the LMS stations in Scotland and thus the eighth largest LMS station. So much for the facts and figures, what specifically made Euston the Premier London station?

In 1939 the ten fastest scheduled LMS passenger trains started or ter-

Left, above: There is always the possibility at terminal stations that the driver approaches too quickly, and accidents happen. In this June 1931 picture we see, on the left, a new type of bufferstop of the Jaeger type, which had recently been installed at Euston. Developed in Germany and designed to absorb heavy shocks, it was generally similar to the normal fixed buffer stop and consisted of a triangular frame supporting a buffer beam at the same level as the locomotive buffers — but instead of being fixed to the rails it was designed to move backwards a short distance if subjected to a very heavy impact. On the right can be seen the hydraulic-type bufferstop normally installed.

Naming ceremonies for locomotives were frequently held at Euston, and on pages 7/8 three such events are illustrated:

Left, below: With the policy of naming locomotives after regiments whose depots (or geographic associations) coincided with the areas covered by the LMS, it became obvious that there were not enough 'Royal Scots' to go round. This remained true even after the batch of 'Scots' which originally carried 'Pioneer locomotive names' had been renamed. As a result, some 'Regimental' names were allocated to unnamed 'Baby Scots' (or 'Patriots' as the LMS chose to call them) and in this picture, taken on April 22 1937, we see No.5504 being named *Royal Signals* with a guard of honour from the Corps on parade. Originally LMS No.5987, nominally rebuilt from a 'Claughton', this new locomotive emerged from Crewe in 1932 and was withdrawn as British Railways No.45504 in March 1962, and immediately cut up for scrap at Crewe works.

minated at Euston. In fact, only three of the first 24 LMS trains in the high speed category were not Euston trains. In terms of distance between stops, 23 out of the 25 LMS passenger trains with long non-stop runs started or finished at Euston. It was factors like these — and many more — that ensured Euston held the premier position.

Euston station began as the London terminus of the London & Birmingham Railway, which opened through-

out on the September 17 1838. The design and layout of the original station can be credited to Robert Stephenson, who was the engineer for the line. Trains had actually started using the station from July 20 1837, when the first southern section of the line was opened and, in order to commemorate their achievement of building the first railway trunk route into the capital, the London & Birmingham Railway commissioned Philip Hardwick to design a triumphal arch

for Euston which became known as the Doric Arch. The completed structure has been described as a propylaeum, which according to the Oxford English Dictionary means:- 'The entrance to a temple or other sacred enclosure, especially when of architectural importance.' All LMS devotees will agree that this is a fitting description for the first picture in this volume about Euston Station, the headquarters of a great railway company which was just that little bit different from the rest of the companies operating in the Kingdom.

It was from London Euston that one travelled direct to the three most important cities in England: Birmingham, Liverpool and Manchester, and by way of Carlisle to Scotland. In addition its routes served Ireland direct, via Holyhead and Fleetwood. Taking all things into consideration Euston was a very important place.

Left: Photographed on July 11 1937 we see 'Royal Scot' 4–6–0 No.6124 *London Scottish*, after presentation by the regiment to the LMS of the regimental crest fixed above the nameplate. In this picture we see Colonel L.D. Henderson MC TD Commanding officer of the London Scottish (14th London Regiment) unveiling the crest after which No.6124 hauled his Battalion to Scotland by special train for a fortnight's training.

Below: Although never in action in a full-blooded sense the Home Guard performed a very valuable service to the country during World War II and it was appropriate to honour these men by naming a locomotive after them. Selected for this purpose was one of the still-unnamed 4–6–0 'Patriots', No.5543 and in this picture, taken during the period that the Battle of Britain was raging on July 30 1940, we see Lt. General Sir Henry Pownall, Inspector General of the Home Guard, about to unveil the *Home Guard* nameplate, with a guard of honour being provided by LMS employees who were members of the local Euston unit. No.5543 was some distance from home when this picture was taken, for at that date it was allocated to Carlisle Upperby (12B). No.5543 was not subsequently rebuilt, and the engine survived until 1962, which was a bad year for the 'Patriots', with almost half the class being withdrawn during these twelve months, including No.5543.

Below, right: This interesting picture was one of a series taken on May 2 1935 to depict the new LMS three-cylinder 4–6–0 No.5552 *Silver Jubilee* at Euston. Described by the reporter covering the event as: "The first of 30 new LMS express locomotives being built at Crewe," No.5552 was compared with the older LNWR 4–4–0 No.5348 *Coronation* seen in this picture. No.5348 held the distinction of being Crewe Works No.5000 whilst its LNWR running number had been No.1800. It was subsequently renumbered 5348, and when this number was required for a new Class 5P5F 4–6–0 it was renumbered 25348 in 1936 and ran thus for a further four years before withdrawal in 1940.

Turning now to No.5552, it should be noted that this engine was not the first of the class. The original No.5552 was built at Crewe in 1934 and construction of this series was into the 5600s when it was decided to take the newly-built No.5642, exchange its identity with the real 5552 and to finish the 'new' 5552 in a very special livery in honour of the Silver Jubilee of King George V. The locomotive was named *Silver Jubilee* and finished in the special livery of glossy black, embellished with polished chromium fittings including hand-rails, boiler bands, steam pipes, reversing reach-rod, top feed cover (the boiler was domeless) and raised LMS letters on the tender and running numbers on the cabside. The 4–6–0 was to retain some of these features for the rest of its life, and when renumbered by British Railways, the new number 45552, which was executed in smaller size numbers than the originals, were nevertheless still in relief and stood proud of the cabside.

The 'Jubilees', unlike most Stanier-designed locomotives, were not an immediate success and considerable problems were encountered in the early years until their design problems were overcome. In essence the original 'Jubilees' were a taper boiler development of the Fowler parallel boiler 'Patriots', but the low-degree superheat domeless boiler fitted to the new 4–6–0s led to numerous problems with the class.

Top: An impressive rear three-quarter view of No.5552 *Silver Jubilee* (formerly No.5642) in absolutely pristine condition, on display at Euston on May 2 1935.

Above: A more conventional view of No.5552, also on May 2 1935.

Left: Taken on April 23 1934 to illustrate the glass windshields then being fitted to assist drivers and firemen, this picture is of great interest as it illustrates the original 5552, which exchanged identity with No.5642 in the spring of the following year. The original No.5552, as No.5642, was named *Boscawen* in 1936, and it survived until 1965 when it was withdrawn as No. BR No.45642. In this picture No.5552 is paired with one of the ten 'high straight-sided' Stanier 3,500-gallon tenders originally coupled to 'Jubilees,' but later paired with other engines.

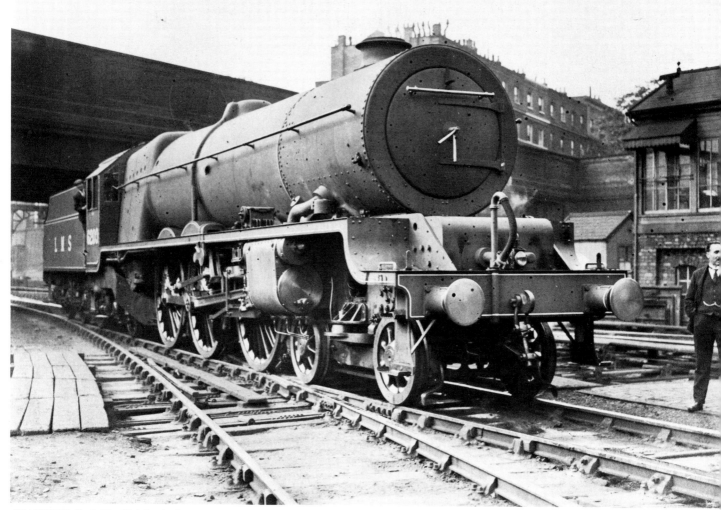

STANIER'S first 'Pacific' is dealt with in greater detail in the Locomotive & Train section, however, here we see pioneer 4–6–2 No.6200 at its official unveiling for the press, at Euston, in June 1933. The original caption, provided by the Topical Press Agency announces: "Secret of Britain's latest and most wonderful railway engine revealed today at Euston." These two pictures depict No.6200, as yet carrying no nameplate on its leading splasher, in original condition with domeless taper boiler and low-degree superheat. In addition, it shows the originally-fitted straight-sided nine-ton 4,000 gallon capacity tender No.9000. This tender was later replaced with curved-sided nine-ton tender No.9065, and subsequently with 10-ton curved-sided tender No.9372. The locomotive was painted in crimson lake livery and the rear view clearly shows the lining applied to No.6200's tender together with the cast-iron plates which are (top to bottom) tender number plate, Crewe Works plate and water capacity plate. No.6200 was subsequently named *The Princess Royal*.

Left: A good clear view of the front of a 'Royal Scot' 4–6–0, prior to the fitting of smoke deflectors, in the charge of Driver J.W. Webster. The '16' shedplate on the smokebox door indicates that the locomotive was based at Longsight, in Manchester. Built at Derby in 1930, No.6164 was named *The Artists Rifleman* and was subsequently rebuilt by British Railways in 1951 with a Type 2A taper boiler. In that form it ran until withdrawal as BR No.46164 in 1962. It was cut up for scrap at Crewe, in March 1963.

Below: The LMS remembered Armistice Day each year and in November 1937 Lady Fraser places a poppy wreath upon an unidentified Stanier 'Pacific' which was ready to haul the 'Royal Scot' express from London to Scotland.

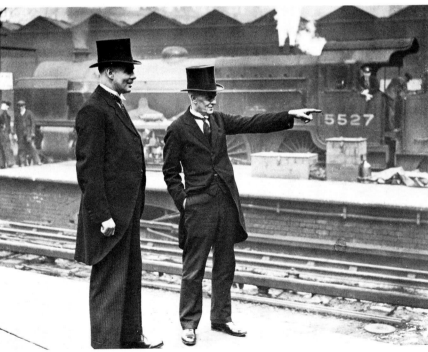

Above, left: Whilst also affording a view of 4–6–0 'Patriot' No.5527 *Southport* in the short-lived 1936 block style lettering, the purpose of taking this photograph was to show the retiring Station Master of Euston, Mr Smith (right), introducing his successor Mr J. Harrison to his new domain on April 9 1937. Certainly their dress is a little different from that worn by modern day British Railways station managers and was probably not too practical for their work. Reverting to No.5527 we have a locomotive that was originally No.5944 when built at Derby in 1933 and which became No.5527 the following year. In 1948 this 'Patriot' was one of the 18 members of the class to be equipped with Type 2A taper boilers and which thus became very similar in appearance to the converted 'Royal Scots'. No.45527 *Southport* was to run until 1964 when it was withdrawn from service by British Railways.

Right: On February 23 1936 'Royal Scot' 4–6–0 No.6154 *The Hussar* sets off on the first leg of a run from London Euston to Edinburgh with a special train chartered by the Royal Covent Garden Opera Company. The load comprised around 200 passengers and 12 truck-loads of scenery — it's a pity we cannot see how the train was made up. No.6154 was a Derby-built 'Royal Scot' and was converted with a Type 2A taper boiler in 1948 and withdrawn from service by British Railways in 1962 as No.46154.

NAMED trains always have that little extra appeal and charisma, and in September 1932 the LMS added a new example to its list. Titled 'The Comet', this was the 11-50am train from London Euston to Manchester and corresponded (according to the reporter of the day) with the 5.40pm up train from Manchester to London Euston. The timing of 'The Comet' from London to Manchester was 3¼ hours, identical with the 'Mancunian', these trains thereby comprising the two fastest services between London and Manchester at that time. Above: station staff attach the train nameboards to an unidentified Period II dining car while (right) un-named 'Royal Scot' 4–6–0 No.6167, which later became the *The Hertfordshire Regiment*, gets to grips with the inaugural service. Rebuilt with a Type 2A taper boiler in 1948, No. 46167 was withdrawn in 1964.

THE 'Midday Scot' from London Euston to Glasgow had until the mid-1930s departed at 1.30pm, arriving at Glasgow at 9.35pm, but this photograph, taken on May 4 1936 shows the start of a retimed service with a later 2.00pm departure but which still maintained a 9.35pm arrival in Glasgow. Hauling the first retimed express is 'Princess Royal' class 4–6–2 No.6212 *Duchess of Kent*, the last locomotive of that class to be built and the only example where the smokebox door was secured by 'dogs' around its circumference. No.6212 retained these 'dogs' at least until 1939, after which it was subsequently fitted with a centrally-mounted screw 'dart'.

Right: May 1932 is the date of this view of Euston station and the occasion was the return of schoolboys from a tour, arriving home at platform No.6. This picture also provides a good view of the Euston overall roof, which sometimes made the station a little gloomy.

Below: Heavy traffic at Euston was not confined to the Summer holiday season and at Christmastime equally heavy traffic could be expected. This atmospheric view, taken on December 23 1931 shows the 'Royal Scot' leaving Euston for Scotland, wreathed in the steam blasting from the cylinder drain cocks. According to the original caption writer the train had to be duplicated (run in two parts) and 'Royal Scot' 4–6–0 No.6110 *Grenadier Guardsman* is probably pulling the main train. Delivered in 1927 by the NBL Co., No.6110 was rebuilt in 1953 by British Railways with a Type 2A taper boiler, in which form it was withdrawn as No.46110 in February 1964.

THE three pictures on this page are all part of the same story and recall the very hard winter of 1947, which was rather more severe than that of 1985/6 which is when these captions were written! In 1947 the country was still recovering from the effects of World War II, fuel was in short supply and life was not easy. We see passengers at Euston (above) leaving the 1.50pm train from Wolverhampton, which left that town on March 5 1947 and was due into Euston at 4.50pm on the same day. However, its actual time of arrival at Euston was 10.00am on March 6! The snow piled on the front of 'Jubilee' 4–6–0 No.5666 *Cornwallis* tells its own story, as indeed does the look on the faces of the passengers who spent around 20 hours on the train which, judging by the exterior of one of the coaches (below) could not have been pleasant. Indeed, the train indicator dated March 6 1947 reads (left): "Special Notice. Indicator Temporary Suspended. Owing to weather conditions trains will be hours late and will be indicated as they approach Euston." It tells the story of some very unhappy journeys.

THE ROYAL SCOT

IF ASKED to nominate the most typical LMS locomotive some people would undoubtedly opt for the Stanier 'Duchess', while others would probably suggest the 'Black' 5, 4–6–0, but in truth it was the 'Royal Scot' 4–6–0 which, more than any other class really typified the LMS in both the pre and post-Stanier periods.

No less an authority than E.S. Cox MI Loco. E. in his paper read before the Institution of Locomotive Engineers on January 2 1946 stated: "A definitely LMS trend of design can be said to have emerged with the 4–6–0 'Royal Scot' and 2–6–4 Tank classes in 1927," and it is of course the 4–6–0s in which we are now interested.

With their roots firmly established in Midland design, the 'Royal Scots' embodied much recent experience, introducing for the first time in combination a higher working pressure and high degree superheat, coupled with long-travel valve gear and bearings which were generously proportioned. In due course they were to become 'new engines' when rebuilt with type 2A taper boilers and other detail modifications. Altered and improved as a result of a conversion programme which commenced with No. 6102 Black Watch in 1943 and was completed with No. 46137 The Prince of Wales's Volunteers (South Lancashire), in 1955, the rebuilt 'Scots' were nevertheless the direct lineal descendants of the original design of 1927.

The early years of the LMS were somewhat dramatic and the story has been told many times before about how, at one point, design work on a compound 'Pacific' was proceeding in the Drawing Office at Derby, while the operating department had managed to persuade the Great Western Railway to lend them one of its 4–6–0 'Castle' class engines to show what a good 4–6–0 was capable of doing. It is of course a matter of history that No 5000 Launceston Castle was put to work between Euston and Crewe and subsequently from Crewe to Carlisle, where it showed its supremacy over all existing LMS types and in particular over the pride of the LNWR, the 'Claughton' 4–6–0s. This class had emerged following the GWR/LNWR locomotive exchange of 1910, but the lessons which ought to have been learned were apparently ignored by LNWR designers and the 'Claughtons' were not as good as they should have been. By 1926, the situation was acute.

The Summer 1927 timetable was to feature a 'showpiece' train on the Anglo-Scottish service, but at the time no LMS locomotive was capable of working the service singlehanded. Design work on the Fowler 'Pacific' was stopped and an attempt was made to build 50 locomotives of the 'Castle' design, but a variety of problems prevented this. The operating Department thus resolved that its needs could be met by a new design of 4–6–0 with three cylinders, maximum size boiler, high-degree superheat and long travel valves. These locomotives, urgently required for the following year were, in effect, to be built 'off the drawing board' by the North British Locomotive Company, Glasgow, which was given the contract to design and build these engines. To assist the NBL Co, a request was made to borrow a complete set of working drawings of the GWR 'Castle' class 4–6–0 from Swindon, but this was ignored or refused. The Southern Railway was more helpful and it loaned the LMS a set of drawings for its new, powerful 'Lord Nelson' class 4–6–0s,

Left: This picture, taken on September 27 1927, the second day of the new service, shows the 'Royal Scot' train arriving at Carlisle behind 4–6–0 No.6127, which was still unnamed, although a backing-plate for a nameplate was already in place on the leading driving wheel splasher. In due course No.6127 was named *Novelty* but later it was renamed *Old Contemtibles*. Originally, it was not intended to name the 'Royal Scots' but fortunately the LMS recognised the value of publicity and public relations and names were bestowed on the class. The principal morning express to Scotland was the 10.00am departure from Euston, and while this train had a long history it did not have a formal name. Couple a new, named locomotive to the train, the LMS reasoned, speed it up, and name the train and you have the essential ingredients for successful 'PR'. All the 'Royal Scot' 4–6–0s were named, therefore, and Nos.6101–6124 were given the names of some of the most famous regiments in the British Army, while the series 6125–49 carried names of pioneer engines from the old Liver-

pool & Manchester Railway, plus other early railways which formed part of the LMS system. The final series of 20 engines, Nos.6150–6169, carried regimental names, with the exception of Nos.6168 and 6169 which became *The Girl Guide* and *The Boy Scout*. Sir Henry Fowler, CME of the LMS, was a keen supporter of the Scout Movement, and no doubt it was felt that if one honoured the boys one must also include the girls, hence the two names for the locomotives at the end of the Derby-built series.

During the 1930s the 'pioneer engine' names were replaced by Regimental names. The Colonels-in-Chief of Regiments not represented within the class probably applied pressure and there were few LMS managers able to argue with any conviction the logic of honouring the old engine names. In any case, there was a splendid ring to all the military names, and the final touch of adding the regimental badge to the nameplate gave added charisma.

Looking now at the train, we find that the leading vehicle is a 50ft all-steel brake van built to diagram D1715, and at this point it is

worth recording that the LMS did not build a special train of vehicles for the new 'Royal Scot' service. It is true that some new designs were first used in the train but they were not specially built for it. A record of the 1927 train formation is not available, but by 1938 it was (from the locomotive): third class brake corridor, third class corridor, third class vestibule, third class vestibule dining car, kitchen car, semi-open first class corridor/vestibule (used for dining), first class brake corridor, vestibule third class. This section went on to Glasgow while the Edinburgh portion comprised: third class vestibule dining coach, kitchen car, semi-open first class corridor vestibule (used for dining), third class vestibule and finally a third class brake corridor.

Finally, it is worth noting that the distant signals in the centre of the picture display the old style of painting with a red front intersected by a vertical white stripe, a white back with vertical black stripe. This was changed to yellow front with a black chevron, and a white back, also with a black chevron.

which had recently been introduced.

Needless to say, close collaboration existed between the NBL Co. and Derby insofar as detailed design was concerned, and a standard Fowler 3,500 gallon tender was to be coupled to this new locomotive. Matters progressed rapidly and the first of the class was despatched to the LMS in July 1927, less than eight months after the letter of intent was signed by the LMS, and the whole batch of 50 locomotives

was rapidly completed by mid-November 1927. This enabled a new 'Royal Scot' train of 415 tons made up to 15 coaches to be introduced on September 26 1927 and worked by the new locomotives which were to run non-stop between Euston and Carlisle. Finally, in 1930 a further 20 locomotives of the class were built at Derby. The first locomotive, No. 6100, was named *Royal Scot* after the train, not the Regiment, and it should be

Above: 'Royal Scot' 4–6–0 class leader No.6100 *Royal Scot* pictured in works grey livery shortly after completion at Glasgow by the North British Locomotive Company, prior to delivery to the LMS.

noted that it carried a 'Royal Scot' smokebox nameplate manufactured and fitted for its American tour.

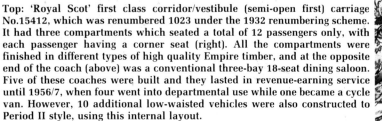

'ROYAL SCOT' ROLLING STOCK

Top: 'Royal Scot' first class corridor/vestibule (semi-open first) carriage No.15412, which was renumbered 1023 under the 1932 renumbering scheme. It had three compartments which seated a total of 12 passengers only, with each passenger having a corner seat (right). All the compartments were finished in different types of high quality Empire timber, and at the opposite end of the coach (above) was a conventional three-bay 18-seat dining saloon. Five of these coaches were built and they lasted in revenue-earning service until 1956/7, when four went into departmental use while one became a cycle van. However, 10 additional low-waisted vehicles were also constructed to Period II style, using this internal layout.

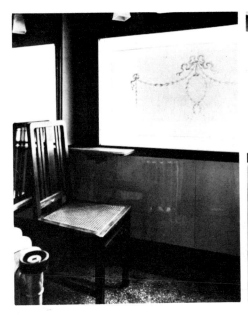

Left: This pair of photographs depict the interior of the toilet-cum-powder room located between the compartments and the open saloon of semi-open first class carriage No.15412, pictured on page 18. Described in 1928 as a 'Mirrored Retiring Room', this compartment was fitted with an ornate patterned window, separate chair, mirror, washbasin and toilet.

Above: First class lounge brake No.15349, photographed in ex-works condition in 1928 for use on the new 'Royal Scot' service. This vehicle became No.5000 under the 1932 renumbering scheme. As with the semi-open first vehicles illustrated these vehicles are often referred to as 'Royal Scot' stock, although they were not specifically built for this service, as five vehicles of each type had entered service in 1928.

Left: Unlike the semi-open first class vehicles, the lounge brakes were not successful in their original form. The high waist-line combined with the rather low-seated armchairs gave a poor view of the passing scenery to all but the tallest passengers. Furthermore, their furnishings were rather sombre. This interior picture illustrates the low seating/high waistline problem, but these vehicles must have nonetheless been very comfortable to travel in. One of the five vehicles built, No.5004, was refitted in 1935 for occasional Royal train use while the four remaining carriages continued running in revenue-earning traffic, before finally being converted to full brakes in 1949/50. They were renumbered 31872–6 and ran for a further 16 years before being withdrawn the mid-1960s.

Right: There was considerable rivalry between the East and West Coast routes for the Anglo-Scottish traffic and in 1928 the LNER announced that it was to start running non-stop between King's Cross and Edinburgh with its 'Pacifics', which had been equipped with corridor tenders to enable crews to be changed mid-way through the journey without stopping the train. Not to be outdone in the publicity stakes, the LMS modified Midland 'Compound' 4–4–0 No.1054's tender by fitting additional, wider coal-rails to increase fuel capacity, and with a special crew on the footplate it ran non-stop from Euston to Edinburgh just before the LNER started its own non-stop service. This picture shows the 'Compound' arriving at Edinburgh Princes Street station on April 28 1928. 'Royal Scot' 4–6–0 No.6113, coupled to a similarly modified tender, worked the Glasgow portion non-stop.

Below: A further attempt to reduce running time between London and Glasgow was made on May 31 1932 and this dramatic picture shows 'Royal Scot' 4–6–0 No.6109 *Royal Engineer* passing Kilburn at speed with one of the accelerated services. By this stage the 'Royal Scots' had been fitted with smoke deflectors, and a variety of experimental types were used in the early years. No.6109 is fitted with an early type of curved-top deflector.

Top: An impressive view of 'Royal Scot' No.6111 *Royal Fuslilier* awaiting the righta-way at Euston with one of the accelerated Anglo-Scottish services of May 1932. The 4–6–0 has a full head of steam and is blowing off very strongly, although as yet the LNWR lower-quadrant signals are still at 'danger'. Note the wooden platform top in this part of Euston, and the corridor gangway boards — used to cover the corridor connection at the rear of a passenger train — leaning against the signal post.

The 'Royal Scot' 4–6–0s enjoyed dominance of the Anglo-Scottish duties for which they were so hurriedly designed for only a short period: they were destined to give way within a few years to Stanier's LMS 'Pacifics', which, in their final form, were without doubt the most effective major express locomotive design to be produced in this country.

Lower: The Topical Press Agency photo-graphers always made the most of these events and in addition to picturing *Royal Fusilier* ready to leave Euston (top) they also witnessed locomotive preparation 'on shed' and in this view Driver Bishop and Fireman Banting, of Camden shed, attend to final lubrication and polishing of the motion for the photographer's benefit. Note the GWR-style crosshead-driven vacuum exhauster, mounted beneath the lower

slide-bar. This device was employed to main-tain the 21in of vacuum in the continuous train brake whilst running — a large ejector was used to create the necessary degree of vacuum, but no small ejectors were fitted at this time.

Eventually the LMS decided that the increased maintenance costs of the crosshead-driven exhausters were excessive and thereafter fitted a secondary small ejector to maintain vacuum 'on the road'.

THE ROYAL SCOT AMERICAN TOUR 1933

IN 1927 the Great Western Railway's 'King' 4–6–0 No.6000 *King George V* had crossed the Atlantic to the United States for the centenary of the Baltimore & Ohio Railroad, and in 1933 No.6100 *Royal Scot* and eight LMS coaches made a similar journey, for exhibition at the Chicago World Fair that year. The locomotive shipped to the USA was not the original No.6100 however, but the newer Derby-built No.6152, with which it exchanged identities. The engine sent to America was fitted with a full set of Stanier-pattern wheels, new driving wheels and axleboxes and a new bogie with brakes.

Above: On April 5 1933 the 'new' 6100's boiler has been lifted from the locomotive frames and is being lowered on to the deck of a large floating crane at Tilbury Dock, from where it was transferred to the hold of the Canadian Pacific's *SS Beaverdale*. The locomotive is clearly in pristine condition and was paired with a large flat-sided Stanier tender, as fitted to the two new Pacifics (Nos.6200/1), then under construction at Crewe.

Right: No.6100's chassis is lifted from the deck of the floating crane, in readiness for loading aboard the *SS Beaverdale*, on the right. Track was laid on the ship's deck to carry the coaches, but the locomotive was almost certainly shipped in the hold.

Left: The *Beaverdale* sailed for Montreal on April 8 1933 and in this view, probably from a crane, the ship is manoeuvred in the dock prior to departure on its trans-Atlantic trip. Somehow one expects a slightly larger ship would have been used, with the result that the coaches appear to be rather precariously placed around the ship's rail. Whilst the coaches sent to the USA were representative of contemporary LMS types, they were not a formation which would normally comprise the 'Royal Scot' train. They were a mixture of three period styles and comprised: 57ft corridor brake first No.5005 (built 1929), 68ft first class sleeping car No.350 (built 1929), 65ft third class sleeping car No.585 (built 1933), 57ft first class brake No.5003 (built 1928), 57ft corridor vestibule car No.1030 (built 1930), 60ft all-electric kitchen-only car No.30073 (built 1933), 60ft vestibule third class dining car No.7764 (built 1932) and 57ft corridor brake third No.5465 (built 1933). The entire LMS coach fleet was renumbered, this scheme starting in 1932, and these vehicles all carried their new numbers, painted in a 'stretched scroll' style unique to this set. The locomotive and train arrived home in time for Christmas on December 5 1933, after an eight month visit to America, in which time No.6100 and its train travelled 11,194 miles.

No.6100 *Royal Scot* is depicted back at work for the LMS, following its return from America. The 4–6–0 is pictured here reunited with a normal Fowler 3,500-gallon tender and carrying the special commemorative nameplate which read: 'This locomotive with the Royal Scot train was exhibited at the Century of Progress exposition, Chicago, 1933, and made a tour of the Dominion of Canada and the United States of America.' During its American tour No.6100 was cared for by Driver W. Gilbertson, Firemen J. Jackson and T. Blackett and Fitter W.C. Woods, and it was inspected by 3,021,601 people. Nos.6100 and 6152 never resumed their original identities.

Right: On December 15 1933 the LMS staged a special ceremony at Euston, with Company Chairman Sir Josiah Stamp presiding, to welcome the 'Royal Scot' train and crew back from their American tour. For its tour No.6100 was fitted with a bell and electric headlight — even a cowcatcher at times. On its return to the United Kingdom the light and cowcatcher were discarded but the famous bell was retained, probably until rebuilding with a taper boiler, in 1950. However, No.6100 is seen here arriving at Euston on December 15 1933 for the 'welcome home' ceremony, still carrying its large headlight. The locomotive is still coupled to its large flat-sided tender, though this was subsequently replaced with a smaller, railed Fowler tender, as illustrated on page 23. In the mid-1930s the class received larger Stanier 4,000 gallon tenders.

The LMS in this period is not normally associated with electric traction, but in this picture the 'Warning Keep off live electric rails' sign draws attention to the LNWR electrified Euston-Watford system. The upper arms on the signal gantry are normal LNWR lower-quadrant 'stop' signals, but they are accompanied by smaller 'calling on' arms beneath the horizontal spar. These small red signals, with a horizontal white stripe, were normally used for engine and stock movements within station limits. A final point of interest is the press photographer crouched at the base of the signal, determined to capture an an impressive low-angle picture of the 4–6–0.

Left: The return of the 'Royal Scot' train from America commanded much press and public attention over Christmas 1933 and into 1934, and the LMS naturally and adroitly capitalised on this interest. No.6100 was despatched on a promotional tour around the LMS system with its train and it is pictured here as the focus of attention at Southend-on-Sea on February 3 1934. No.6100 is preserved in rebuilt form at the Bressingham Steam Museum painted in LMS crimson lake, a livery it never carried at any time in rebuilt form.

THE camera never lies! In these years the news agencies did not hesitate to manipulate the photographic images of the day, to produce a given effect, or create a particular story. The upper picture on this page is a quite genuine picture of Stanier 'Princess Royal' 4-6-2 No.6207 *Princess Arthur of Connaught* heading north with 'The Royal Scot' on June 11 1936, near Rugby. However, the Topical Press Agency artist was set to work to produce the composite picture below, which seemed to be designed to show that speed and technological progress should be kept in perspective. The original caption, under the heading 'NOT SO FAST — BUT GETS THERE JUST THE SAME', reads: "An unusual picture affording a study in contrast. Taken as the famous LMS 'Royal Scot' flashed through Brinklow, near Rugby, where the Oxford canal runs alongside the main line. A barge, laden with goods, represents the commercial transport of a less speedy age, while the 'Royal Scot' roaring past on its way to the North, illustrates the pace of our present machine-ruled times." No.6207 was one of the second series of Stanier's 'Pacifics', which carried the number series 6203–6212; all were built at Crewe in 1935.

Above: Although taken on February 15 1948, just into the period of British Railways ownership, this picture is purely LMS in essence. On that day in austerity Britain, still recovering from the effects of World War II, it was decided to resume the pre-war name of 'The Royal Scot' for the 10.00am departure from Euston to Glasgow and Edinburgh. The February 15 date for this resumption of service was chosen because it was the 100th anniversary of the completion of through railway communication by the West Coast route between London Euston and Glasgow and Edinburgh. The inaugural 'Royal Scot' of February 15 1948 is shown here skimming the water troughs at Bushey, Herts as it speeds north behind No.6245 *City of London*, painted in the 1946 LMS express passenger livery of black with a 2½in maroon band flanked by a ⅜in straw line on each side running along the footplate angle. Additional straw-maroon-straw lining appeared on the cylinders and steam chest casing, cabside and tender sides, while the company ownership markings and numbers were of the Gill Sans type painted in straw with a maroon line all round, leaving a straw margin on the outside.

Right: Without doubt the passenger train guard of old was — or could be — a formidable character and in this picture we see two LMS guards who were born on the same day, January 18 1872, and who both retired on their 65th birthday, in 1937, the day after this picture was taken. According to the original captions the guards, known as 'the twins', were well known to hundreds of regular travellers between London and Glasgow. Albert Edward Higgins (left) entered the service as a boy messenger at Bletchley in 1886 and had been a main line guard at Euston for 36½ years. George Kemp (right) also started with the London & North Western Railway, but in his case service did not begin until 1890. Between them they claimed nearly 100 years of combined railway service and over 8,000,000 miles by train.

THE
STREAMLINERS

DURING the mid 1930s business throughout the world began to improve and as a consequence the competition to rail services increased. This competition to rail came mostly from road transport, for as yet air travel was still in its infancy although it could be seen as becoming an important factor in the years to come. There was of course competition also from the other railways of which the LNER was the most important. Probably the most important railway trunk route in the UK was from London to Scotland, and while the LMS owned two routes (the West Coast or old LNWR/CR route from London Euston to Glasgow and Edinburgh and the old MR/GSWR route to Glasgow from London St Pancras it was the LNWR/CR link that provided the principal artery along which majority of passenger traffic flowed.

The rival route was the East Coast line from London Kings Cross to Edinburgh, via the GNR/NER/NBR lines, operated by the LNER. This Railway was highly motivated in a publicity sense and its exploits with the 'Flying Scotsman' express are well known, and are extensively illustrated in 'LNER Reflections', companion volume to this book. Indeed the introduction by the LNER of its streamlined 'A4 Pacifics' to work its latest Anglo-Scottish trains in 1935, had caught the public imagination. The streamlined locomotives of both LNER and LMS designs presented an impressive sight, although it is doubtful if under identical conditions a streamlined locomotive would be faster or more efficient than its unstreamlined sister. In fact, it has become generally accepted that to achieve the benefit of streamlining one needs a really long, continuous high-speed run to achieve a major benefit and in any case, it took the vast expenditure of the 1960s which preceded the 100mph electric trains operating out of Euston to provide a track upon which any real benefits from streamlining would have been achieved as far as the LMS design was concerned.

However, by 1937 the public had caught the streamlining 'craze' and from the publicity standpoint it made sense to ensure that these latest LMS 4–6–2s were streamlined. Therefore, it was decided to fit an aerodynamic casing for the new 'Pacifics' and to adopt a spectacular livery for the locomotive and train both designed to project the image of high speed. Without doubt, the final streamlined shape

Below: The pioneer 'Princess Coronation Pacific,' No.6220 *Coronation*, stands with the new train at Crewe. The normal service commenced on July 5 1937 and it was No.6220 which achieved a speed of 114 mph descending Madeley Bank in 1937 whilst working the press run of the 'Coronation Scot'. Two years later No.6220 exchanged identities with No.6229 *Duchess of Hamilton* for its American visit in 1939, although the 'Pacific' reverted to its original identity in 1943 on its return to Britain. As No.6220 again she spent much of her life at Polmadie (Glasgow) and with an average annual mileage of 58,741 she was withdrawn from service in April 1963.

evolved by the LMS designers for the 'Princess Coronations' was one which caught the public eye in no uncertain fashion.

Design work for this high speed train proceeded through 1936 with a planned introduction date of 1937. Work proceeded apace while LMS Chief Mechanical Engineer William Stanier was away in India, as part of a team of engineers investigating the riding characteristics of certain Indian Railway 4–6–2s. However, in his absence, his design team 'delivered the goods' in style and the new locomotives, officially called 'The Princess Coronation' class, but more usually known to the enthusiast as 'Duchesses' and to the railwaymen who worked them as 'Big Lizzies', were a success from the outset.

Gone was the earlier Stanier interest in low-superheat boilers, this class was fitted with a 40-element superheater of 856sq. ft. — the largest superheating surface ever provided on any British locomotive. Compared

with the 'Princess Royal' 4–6–2s, the driving wheel diameter was increased by 3in. to 6ft. 9in. and the cylinder diameter increased by ¼in. to 16¼in. The outside cylinders were brought forward and the influence of the GWR 'King' 4–6–0 design, seen on Stanier's 'Princess Royal' 'Pacifics', disappeared.

One could write endlessly about this class of 38 locomotives, which were popular engines with footplatemen and observers alike. The pictures we have for this volume feature the two original series of 10 engines in their 'as built' condition. However, before turning to these pictures we should perhaps consider the trains which they were to haul.

Writing in the September 20 1938 issue of 'The Times', which included a London Midland & Scottish Railway Centenary number, Naomi Royde-Smith described her travels on the Coronation Scot train: "Consisting of three nine-coach trains", she wrote, "that one, upholstered in blue, leaves

Above: Taken on the day that it emerged from Crewe works (May 25 1937), this publicity photograph of No.6220 *Coronation* provides an interesting comparison with a reproduction of Stephenson's famous *Rocket*, of 1830. The two locomotives represent more than a century of steam locomotive development and yet in essence they are very similar in their utilisation of blastpipe exhaust via a smokebox, and drive by a simple reciprocating mechanism. Although various locomotive designers (including Stanier) built locomotives which departed from this basic principle, utilising turbine drive, miniaturised enclosed valve gears and water-tube marine-type boilers, they were never extensively duplicated across the country and the Stephensonian concept was followed by British Railways to the very end of steam construction with Robert Riddles' 9F 2–10–0 No.92220 *Evening Star*, at Swindon, in 1960.

Facing page: A very impressive elevated view of No.6220 *Coronation* at its official unveiling at Crewe works, in May 1937.

Euston at 1.30pm daily except Saturdays while the other, upholstered in green, leaves Glasgow at the same hour and that they pass each other at

Above: The wild slopes of Shap Fell, in Westmorland, make the perfect setting for this class and here we see No.6221 *Queen Elizabeth* during 1937 climbing un-assisted past Shap Wells with a northbound train of nine coaches. No.6221 was unique in so far that she was the only member of the blue series (6220–4) to be repainted in the crimson lake livery, in 1941. Withdrawn in May 1963 *Queen Elizabeth* achieved an average annual mileage of 58,162.

Right: The narrow, wooden-decked platform at Euston is filled with well-wishers as the driver of No.6220 *Coronation* gets under way, probably with the first 'Coronation Scot' service train of July 5 1937.

Preston, arriving at their destinations at 8.00pm ... The third train, upholstered in brown, is a spare but is used to relieve the strain imposed upon the other two by doing two or three trips each week." She continued: "One of the trains is veneered with wood cut from the piles of old Waterloo Bridge, seasoned by 120 years immersion in the mud of the River Thames, as a tablet makes known to the traveller." She makes a further interesting remark concerning the dress of the 'guard' and suggests that instead of the dark blue and gold braid of the other trains, the man 'in charge' of the Coronation Scot wore pale blue and silver. She was of course confusing the guard with the conductor or attendant. A remarkable description of her journey is contained in this issue of 'The Times' and is worthy of reading by those with a deep interest in seeing how the public saw what was happening on the LMS at that time.

We can now turn to the coaches themselves, and it is perhaps a little surprising that the vehicles which made up these trains were mostly not brand new but reconditioned vehi-cles, albeit of the latest type. It has been suggested that permission to 'build' special trains was only granted under the strict condition that the costs should be kept to a minimum. As previously mentioned, three sets were provided and the train composition was: Brake First Corridor, First Corridor, Semi-Open First, Kitchen Car, Semi-Open Third, Semi-Open Third, Kitchen Car, Semi-Open Third, Brake Third. Most of the coaches selected for the sets were taken from the latest batches of new stock which had just gone into service. The coaches were completely refitted internally however, except for the kitchen car, were equipped with a pressure heating and ventilation system. Because there were no suitable Corridor First or First Brakes available, these vehicles were newly built for the service. Within the train, the first class compartments seated two-a-side while the third class vehicles sat three each side, and although in some respects the interiors were less modern than their LNER counterparts they probably did not date quite so quickly.

Above: Photographed on November 10 1938 this picture was taken at Camden locomotive shed on the occasion that a party of German Editors visited the depot. Two members of the class are 'on shed' and whilst the 'Pacific' steaming past the visitors cannot be identified, the locomotive on the right is No.6226 _Duchess of Norfolk_. This locomotive, like 15 other members of the class, never exchanged their original tenders. No.6226 ran with tender No.9744 and its home shed, from 1946, tended to be Carlisle Upperby. Withdrawn in September 1964, No.46226's average annual recorded mileage was 67,764.

The LMS was determined to extract the maximum publicity from the introduction of its streamlined 'Pacifics', thus, on June 29 1937 the LMS staged a test run from Euston with the new No.6220 *Coronation*. Above, left: Driver T.J Clarke oils round his locomotive prior to the run for the benefit of the Topical photographer, and, as might be expected, the locomotive is in very clean condition with not a speck of dirt or drop of spilt oil to be seen anywhere around the wheels, frames and motion. During this run No.6220 achieved a speed of 106.5mph on a five-mile stretch between Whitmore and Crewe, including a maximum of 114mph down the bank at Madeley — which wrested the world speed record for steam traction from the LNER — though Gresley 'A4' *Mallard* reclaimed this permanently with its 126 mph sprint of 1938.

Clearly pleased with their performance, Crewe's Driver T.J. Clarke and Fireman J. Lewis are congratulated at Euston by LMS Chief Mechanical Engineer William A. Stanier. Driver Clarke's train of eight coaches weighed 263 tons (tare) and 270 tons (gross) and it was a tribute to his locomotive handling skills — and the engine's design — that despite the fact that Crewe was only a few miles ahead when the maximum speed was recorded, he nevertheless managed to negotiate the crossovers into the station without serious mishap, though it was reported that the dining car required some new crockery! The average Euston-Crewe speed had been 73.1 mph. See also page 2.

Facing page, top right: 'Princess Coronation' class leader No.6220 *Coronation* is the focus of attention at Euston on June 29 1937, following the return run of its record-breaking trip to Crewe when it achieved 114mph. Note the very wide variety of hats being worn by the spectators: everything from school caps to top hats!

Right: On June 8 1938 'Princess Coronation' No.6225 *Duchess of Gloucester*, the first locomotive of the second series (in crimson lake, with gold lining) departs from Euston in fine style with a special train for Glasgow. Conveying 120 'locomotive experts' attending the summer meeting of the Institution of Locomotive Engineers, the train was timed to depart from Euston at 9.50am and arrive at Glasgow at 4.45pm. No.6225 was to achieve an annual mileage of 66,183 before withdrawal in September 1964 and held the distinction of accumulating the highest recorded mileage for any member of the class, namely 1,742,624 miles.

Below: No.6226 *Duchess of Norfolk* was the second locomotive of the 6225–6229 series, built in 1938. Unlike the first five blue and silver liveried locomotives, this series was painted in crimson lake with gold lines and so formed a closer visual match to the majority of the LMS coaches which they were likely to haul. Achieving an annual average recorded mileage of 67,764, No.46226 was withdrawn in September 1964. With the steam sanders helping adhesion, No.6226 storms out of Euston with an Anglo-Scottish express.

Right: An early publicity photograph, taken on June 23 1937, shows the driver and fireman of No.6220 with some interested lady onlookers at Euston — even the locomotive headlamps were 'winged' to emphasise the speedy characteristics of the 'Streamliners'. Note the highly polished finish of the locomotive, and its recessed drawhook.

Below: The LMS established a custom of placing poppy garlands on some of its locomotives on Remembrance Day each year and in this picture we see Mr J. Harrison, the Euston Station Master, placing a poppy garland on the front of 'Princess Coronation' No.6224 *Princess Alexandra* at Euston on November 11 1939. No.6224 was the last member of the original five blue and silver engines and had the unrivalled distinction of undergoing more boiler changes than any other member of the class — 11 in all.

Left: In 1937 the LMS had decided that at the 1939 New York World Fair it would exhibit a complete 'Coronation Scot' locomotive and train and the engine selected was No.6229 *Duchess of Hamilton*, which then exchanged identities with No.6220 *Coronation*. Thus disguised as No.6220 *Coronation*, No.6229 was equipped with both a bell and an electric headlight, to conform with American operating regulations. Here we see Driver F.C Bishop, of London, and Fireman J. McKinnon Carswell, of Scotland, inspecting the new fittings at Euston in January 1939, prior to departure.

Below: Complete with its winged headlamps 'No.6220' parades for the press at Euston in January 1939. The locomotive and train was painted in the crimson and gold livery.

Left: The locomotive and train were shipped to New York from Southampton aboard the *SS Belpamela* and in this picture a group of dock workers fix a greeting to the side of first class sleeping car No.377, though it is probably safe to assume this was for the benefit only of the press: it is difficult to believe that a banner such as this would have survived much Atlantic weather! The sides of the coach appear to have been heavily greased, to protect the paintwork.

Above: After being towed onto the dockside at Southampton on what appears to be temporary track, the 105-ton 'Pacific' is swung aboard the *SS Belpamela*, in readiness for lowering into the ship's hold, on January 20 1939.

Right: Four of the 'Coronation Scot' coaches, lashed on the deck of the *SS Belpamela*, ready for departure for New York. The LMS originally intended to exhibit a 1937 train but as the Chief Operating Manager pointed out: "This would not be possible without detriment to our ordinary business", and so in November of that year it was decided to build a completely new train. Considerable internal debate followed but the formation eventually sent to the USA comprised: brake first corridor and first corridor (articulated); semi-first corridor (with cocktail lounge) and first open diner (articulated); kitchen car and third open diner (articulated); first class sleeper; third class brake. Six of the eight vehicles were articulated therefore, and all but the first class sleeping car were newly-built for the exhibition. Together with No.6229, disguised as No.6220 *Coronation*, this train toured the USA from March 21 to April 14 1939 and during this time it covered 3,121 miles. After the tour the locomotive was exhibited at the New York World Fair and it was still there in September 1939, when World War II broke out. While the coaches remained in the USA until after the end of the war, No.6220 was returned home in 1943, when it resumed its former identity as No.6229. Without doubt, as BR No.46229, and today preserved at the NRM in main line working order, this locomotive is now the most photographed member of the class.

Above: A very interesting photograph of No.6229, masquerading as No.6220 *Coronation*, during its American tour with its 'Coronation Scot' train. The crimson-liveried 'Pacific' is pictured on Thomas Viaduct, Belroy, Maryland alongside the USA's contemporary 'Royal Blue' streamlined express train. The picture strongly emphasises the altogether larger American loading gauge. Located on the Baltimore & Ohio Railroad's main line from Baltimore to Washington, this viaduct was built in 1835 and was 700ft long with eight 60ft arches, which carried the railway 65ft above the river. The picture was taken on March 30 1939.

Left: We conclude this look at the 'streamliners' with this August 16 1943 picture, showing volunteers cleaning LMS locomotives during their spare time. It was recorded that about 800 volunteers at 38 depots cleaned 300 locomotives on a single day. Here we see a team of five people, including one woman cleaning No.6240 *City of Coventry* which is still in LMS red and gold livery, albeit under a thick layer of grime. Spending most of its life as a Camden engine, BR No.46240 was withdrawn from service in September 1964, with an average annual mileage of 70,949 to its credit. The 4–6–2 was scrapped at Cashmore's yard, Great Bridge, in December 1964.

LOCOMOTIVES AND TRAINS

ON January 1 1923 the LMS came into being as the largest joint-stock company operating a transport system in the world. It owned 10,316 locomotives of 393 different types and within this total there were only 1,882 superheated locomotives, even though the value of high-degree superheating had been accepted for the past 12 years at least.

The new CME of the LMS was George Hughes, who had been CME of the Lancashire & Yorkshire Railway since 1904, subsequently becoming CME of the 'enlarged LNWR', which amalgamated with the LYR in 1922, one year before the 'Big Four' Grouping of 1923. In the all-important consideration of seniority, Hughes had outranked Beames, the LNWR CME, this assuring his promotion.

According to ES Cox M.I. Loco E., in his paper read to the Institution of Locomotive Engineers on January 2 1946, the urgent motive power need on the West Coast route was for a main line passenger class, a large passenger tank locomotive and a

heavy freight engine. The first requirement was met by the superheated conversion of Hughes' earlier four-cylinder 4–6–0 class but unfortunately this design did not prove to be suitable for general use on the Anglo-Scottish passenger service. A number of these locomotives were employed working trains on the Carlisle-Crewe section, but their performance was not entirely satisfactory.

It was at first thought that the large passenger tank requirement could be met by the new design of 4–6–4T, and it was planned to build 60 examples, but when it was realized that their size limited their widespread use only 10 were completed and the material

on hand for a further 20 examples was used to construct tender locomotives.

The final requirement for a large goods engine was really intended for the Midland Division, which urgently required a locomotive to do the work currently performed by 0–6–0s working in pairs. The route from Nottinghamshire to London carried the heaviest mineral traffic on the LMS, but this old Midland Railway route did have severe weight and width restrictions which prevented the desired designs being introduced. Nevertheless the requirement was met in part by the 2–6–0+0–6–2 Garratts introduced in 1927 and the 0–8–0s built between 1929 and 1932.

THE 2–6–0+0–6–2 Beyer Garratt type developed for the LMS was impressive in appearance, even if the locomotive's performance fell short of expectations. The huge firebox struck fear into many young firemen charged with the task of providing the steam required to keep heavy trains rolling.

Although the LMS 'Garratts' spent most of their time on the Nottinghamshire-London coal trains, returning north with empty wagons, they were also employed on the shorter run from Toton to Washwood Heath (Birmingham) and whilst they did not (as far as known) travel west of Birmingham in LMS days, they did venture onto 'the Bristol road' during the British Railways period.

The 2–6–0+0–6–2 type had sprung from a need by the LMS to provide a locomotive which would eliminate the double-heading of London-bound coal trains from the yards at Toton. For many years the Midland Railway had employed nothing larger than '4F' 0–6–0s, working in pairs, and as a consequence the LMS developed the Garratt type in conjunction with the Beyer-Peacock company. The story has been told before (notably by E.S. Cox in 'Locomotive Panorama') about how discussions were being held at the same time between Beyer Peacock and several different, and quite independent offices of the LMS about this project! Suffice to say that the influence of the former Midland Railway Company ensured that the worst possible options were adopted, with the result that the class was

bedevilled by design faults. The worst of these were short-travel valve gear, together with axle boxes of insufficient bearing size, which led to overheating.

Three prototypes were built in 1927 and No.4997 was the first example built. The other two engines were Nos. 4998/9. Following three years trials with this trio, a further 30 engines were built in 1930, and numbered 4967-4996. Comparisons revealed that a single 2–6–0+0–6–2 did not burn any less coal than a pair of '4F' 0–6–0s, but the use of one of these massive engines meant that only a single footplate crew was required, thus saving two wages.

The original three engines differed in detail from the batch of 30 built in 1930. Nos. 4997-9 were built with fixed coal bunkers of seven tons capacity, while the water tanks at each end of the locomotive held 4,700 gallons. The later series had a nine-ton coal capacity and carried 4,500 gallons of water. During 1932/3 the later series were equipped with 10-ton capacity rotary bunkers and the prototype nine-ton capacity bunker originally fitted to 4986 was transferred to 4997. In 1938 the class was renumbered 7997-7999, and at Nationalisation British Railways added 40,000 to the class numbers, to give the range 47997-47999. As BR No.47997, this locomotive survived until withdrawal in February 1956, from Hasland MPD. The class became extinct in April 1958 with the withdrawal of No.47994 (LMS Nos. 4994/7994), also from Hasland.

Right: Lancashire & Yorkshire Railway Hughes class 5 4–6–0 No.1672, built in June 1923, the first year of the LMS regime. The locomotive was one of a batch built to a LYR order and, interestingly, the locomotive carried its pre-Grouping number on a cabside plate of LYR style, but lettered LM&SR, as were the whole series 1665–78. The first six engines of the class (Nos.1659–64) had LYR-style numberplates lettered LNWR/LYR, as a consequence of their amalgamation in 1922. The final engines of the class, while allocated LYR numbers 1679–83, entered traffic as LMS Nos.10450–4, and never carried pre-Grouping numbers. No.1672, shown here, became LMS No.10443 and carried full crimson lake livery. It survived until withdrawal in 1936.

Left, above: Following the Grouping of 1923 the LMS had urgent need of a large passenger tank class and it was initially believed that the new LYR 'Baltic' — one of the last Horwich designs — would fulfil the role. Changing motive power needs prompted a change of plan and only ten of the originally-planned 30 examples were built, the final 20 being constructed as 4–6–0s. Developed from the superheated Walschaerts valve gear-fitted rebuilds of the original Hughes 4–6–0s, these massive 4–6–4Ts were amongst the biggest passenger tanks ever built for British use. This picture shows No.11114 (the class was numbered 11110–9) in highly polished condition on display at the Wembley Exhibition of 1925. The engine having doubtless passed through the paintshop before going to London. This class, although not unsuccessful, was not particularly long-lived: as a small group the engines did not fare well in the LMS standardisation policy. The first withdrawal occurred in 1938, No.11114 survived until 1941 and the class was made extinct with the withdrawal of No.11110 in 1942.

Left, below: The third major motive power requirement of the newly-formed LMS in 1923 was for a heavy freight locomotive. This was in part filled by the 2–6–0+0–6–2 (illustrated opposite), while the new 0–8–0 design was in essence a 'Midlandised' version of the final form of 0–8–0 built by the LNWR. The LMS took the basic design of the LNWR G1/G2 and standardised an improved version, fitted with smaller cylinders than the LNWR design, but coupled with a 20psi increase in boiler pressure, to 200psi. Inside long-travel Walschaerts valve gear was provided, together with a redesigned front end, but these improvements were compromised by the chassis, whose chief weakness was its class 4F bearings which were undersized for an engine of this size. This created problems in traffic, with overheated bearings occurring and low mileages recorded between repairs. Consequently, the class did not enjoy a long life and withdrawal began in 1949, with the class becoming extinct in 1962. This picture shows No.9599 at Crewe Works on December 16 1929, photographed in works grey as the 100th locomotive built that year. The original caption claimed that the year's production at the works weighed 5,550 tons, with a new locomotive being completed every 2¼ working days!

Right: Pioneer Stanier 'Pacific' No.6200 *The Princess Royal*, pictured at Euston during a period of dynamometer car testing, with a 500-ton train. Mr. E.J.H. Lemon, a Vice President of the LMS, was involved in these tests and is seen here on the footplate on August 15 1933. The 'Princess Royal' class was introduced in 1933 when it became apparent that while the 'Royal Scot' 4–6–0s were putting up some good performances with trains of around 420 tons, there was a need for a larger locomotive which would not only be powerful enough to work a 500-ton train, but which would be capable of working through from London Euston to Glasgow with only a change of engine crew required, at Carlisle. The need was pressing and when W.A Stanier took over as CME of the LMS on January 1 1932 this requirement must have been virtually the top priority, because by April of that year two basic schemes had been prepared for consideration. These new Stanier proposals owed something to the unfulfilled 'Pacific' projects initiated by Stanier's predecessors; firstly George Hughes, who considered three and four-cylinder simple expansion locomotives, and Sir Henry Fowler, who envisaged a four-cylinder 'Compound' design. The initial Stanier proposals were also for both three and four-cylinder simple expansion designs, and it is probable that it was Stanier, coming from the Great Western, which had adopted either two or four cylinders as its standard, who had ensured that to the successful 'Royal Scot' three-cylinder formula was added an alternative four-cylinder proposal.

In 1932, three four-cylinder 4–6–2s were ordered for the 1933 locomotive building programme but it was subsequently announced that the third locomotive was to be a non-condensing turbine design, although it was made clear that this locomotive must include as many standard parts as possible. The first two engines, Nos.6200 and 6201, named *The Princess Royal* and *Princess Elizabeth*, were completed in 1933 but turbine-driven No.6202 was not ready until 1935. Unlike the previous two 'Pacifics', No.6202 was not named, although unofficially it was always known as the 'Turbomotive'.

The design of the two original locomotives varied a little from the later second series. While the cylinder layout, with its two inside cylinders mounted well forward, driving the leading coupled axle (similar to the GWR

'King' class, with which Stanier had, in his GWR days been closely associated) remained identical for both series, the second series (Nos.6203–12) had a different main steam pipe arrangement at its connection to the inside cylinders. Probably more important was the boiler. The pioneer pair were equipped with domeless boilers, with a Swindon-style low degree superheater, but in due course it was realised that this did not suit LMS operating conditions. This led to an increase in the number of superheater elements, together with an increase in the firebox heating surface provided by creating a combustion chamber in the forward part of the firebox.

Other variations between the first and second series of 'Pacifics' included lubrication arrangements and in particular the tenders — the most obvious visual difference. The original tenders built with Nos.6200 and 6201 were

to a new design. Carrying nine tons of coal and 4,000 gallons of water they were inspired by the contemporary Fowler 3500-gallon flat-sided tender which, at best, carried only 5½ tons of coal. The extra capacity of the new design was achieved by lengthening the tender, which although six-wheeled ran with a 15ft wheelbase, 2ft longer than the Fowler design. Three tenders of this type were built, and the third vehicle, intended for No.6202 was used by No.6100 *Royal Scot* during its North American Tour. Unfortunately, the design was less than satisfactory — it was not self-trimming for example (coal did not work down by gravity and vibration to the shovelling plate) — and this led to the provision of the Stanier high-sided tender, which had inward-curved upper platework. The second series received these new Stanier 4,000-gallon tenders from the outset ⁖ Nos.6200/6201 received replacements.

Left: The LMS large passenger tank requirement was met initially by the Fowler 2–6–4T class (Nos.2300–2424), built between 1927 and 1934. Following Stanier's arrival, a taper boiler version of the Fowler design was produced in 1934, and the first examples to enter traffic were three-cylinder engines, Nos.2500–2536. It was believed that three cylinders gave more rapid acceleration, but in service it was found that there was no real advantage over the two-cylinder design and the three-cylinder version was not multiplied further. This picture shows No.2500, the first of the three-cylinder 2–6–4Ts, at Euston as part of a display of locomotives and rolling stock staged in April 1934. Although built for the London Tilbury & Southend section, the class did not go straight to work on this line as bridge strengthening was incomplete. From 1935, however, all 37 engines remained on the LT&S, except for a short period during the war, when services on this line were drastically reduced. Withdrawal began in 1960 and the class was extinct by 1962, when the electrification from Fenchurch Street to Shoeburyness was completed. No.2500 is preserved as part of the National Collection, at the Bressingham Steam Museum.

Left: The third member of the original trio of 'Pacifics' was No.6202, the 'Turbomotive', seen here at Euston on June 27 1935, being inspected by the driver, together with LMS CME William A. Stanier (left) and LMS President Sir Josiah Stamp (right). The contemporary caption describes No.6202 simply as a 'two-funnelled engine', which indicates a marked lack of media understanding about this unusual locomotive! In all respects No.6202 was an experimental locomotive which was noteworthy for its long life. In 1932 Stanier had visited Sweden, where he had been impressed to see a non-condensing turbine locomotive of the Ljungstrom type at work Consequently, the Company decided to cancel its order for the third original 'Princess Royal' 4–6–2 and build in its place a non-condensing turbine locomotive. The new engine's boiler, wheels and frames would be similar to the 'Princess Royal' class, but there the similarity ended. A contract for turbine equipment was placed with Metropolitan Vickers and No. 6202 eventually cost £15, 210 — 1½ times of the price of the second series of 'Princess Royals'

Right: A rear-three quarter vies of No.6202 at Euston, also on June 27 1935, from the driver's side. The principle of turbine drive was that it provided a more consistent torque on the driving axle, eliminating the hammer-blow normally associated with conventional locomotives employing cylinders and reciprocating valve motion. No.6202 was fitted with two turbines, the long one on the left of the locomotive (shown here) was used for forward running, while the much smaller turbine located on the right side was for reverse. No.6202 presented a very neat design, especially from the left hand side.

Right, above: Framed by an impressive array of LNWR lower quadrant signals, No.6202 performs a 'run-past' for the press cameras at Camden, giving a good view of the smaller 'reverse' turbine housing. After intensive trials on the Anglo-Scottish passenger services, when it was compared with the other members of the 'Princess Royal' class, the 'Turbomotive' settled down to regular work on the Euston-Liverpool service. It was however taken out of traffic between September 1939 until July 1941, and again between 1943 and 1944, before being finally withdrawn as a turbine locomotive in March 1950, after completing 458,772 miles in service. The 1935 batch of 'Princess Royals' had by this time recorded an average nearer to 750,000 miles. No.6202 lay dismantled in Crewe works until May 1951, when British Railways decided that no further work on turbine transmission should be undertaken and in 1952 the decision was made to rebuild the 'Turbomotive' in conventional form.

At a cost of £8,875, No.46202, now named *Princess Anne*, re-entered service on August 15 1952. It was unique. The front end of the new frames were of the 'Coronation' pattern, modified at the front end to suit the 'Princess Royal' type platform. In addition, the 'Coronation' layout was used for the valve motion and the original boiler was re-installed, but altered to give a larger superheating surface: a new smokebox was also added. The original cab permitted modification to accept the reversing gear and additionally, the driving wheels now had balance weights. Coupled to its old tender, No.46202, as sole example of 'The Princess Anne' class, ran for only a few weeks before it was involved in the tragic Harrow disaster of October 8 1952. Officially withdrawn from stock in May 1954, the former 'Turbomotive' was subsequently cut up for scrap, only the boiler being retained.

Right, below: A group of onlookers divide their interest between the 'Topical' photographer and the Ljungstrom turbine locomotive tested in the 1920s by the LMS, after arrival at St Pancras. Throughout the history of steam traction attempts were made to improve on the original Stephenson concept — usually without too much success. In the early 1920s co-operation between Beyer Peacock and the Swedish Ljungstrom company led to the construction in Britain of this unique locomotive, which ran for the first time on LNER tracks in July 1926. Two months later trials began on the LMS, working semi-fast services linking Derby and Manchester. Following modifications it was employed in 1927 on heavier trains between Derby and St Pancras, where it achieved speeds of 85mph, and used 84% less water than the newly-built 'Crab' 2–6–0s in similar conditions! The British loading gauge prevented the full potential of the design being exploited and, probably more significantly, the initial cost (in the case of the prototype at least) was six times more than a conventional engine and little further progress was made. This engine remained intact until the 1950s and Beyer Peacock doubtless hoped that one day interest in steam turbine drive would be revived, but this never happened.

Caption overleaf

Previous page & Right: Splendid comparative views of LNWR 'Jumbo' 2–4–0 No.5031 *Hardwicke* and 'Royal Scot' 4–6–0 No.6118 *Royal Welch Fusilier*, which highlight the increasing dimensions of West Coast motive power. The picture particularly emphasises how boilers had increased significantly in both length and diameter. *Hardwicke* was built in 1892 as a renewal of an earlier 2–4–0 and in 1895 it was a member of the group of 256 2–4–0s collectively known as 'Jumbos'. As in the Grouping era, intense rivalry between the East and West Coast routes had led to 'races' from London to Scotland and the years 1888 and 1895 were very much 'racing years', with the latter year witnessing an epic feat by *Hardwicke*. The scene had been set in 1895 by the acceleration of the West Coast 8.00pm express, timed to arrive at Aberdeen at 7.40am, rather than the previous 7.50am, the extra 10 minutes providing more time to transfer passengers and luggage to the connecting GNSR Deeside train. The challenge was taken by the East Coast route and the 'racing' really got under way when the West Coast train was advertised as arriving at Aberdeen at 7.00am, in August. Developments followed quickly, trains were divided and the timetable was apparently abandoned and whilst one can appreciate the intense excitement this prompted amongst the railway staff, one also wonders what kind of ride some unsuspecting passengers endured. The final 'race' took place on August 22/23

when the West Coast train arrived at Aberdeen at 4.32am — 540 miles from Euston covered in 512 minutes. No.790 *Hardwicke's* contribution was to work the train between Crewe and Carlisle, a distance of 141 miles, in 126 minutes, start-to-stop. This represented an average speed of 67mph — a record which stood for more than 41 years, until 1936, when Stanier 'Princess Royal' 4–6–2 No.6201 *Princess Elizabeth* during trials covered the same distance pass-to-pass in 122 min 37 sec. In fairness, it must be admitted that *Hardwicke's* load was a comparatively featherweight 75 tons, but it was nevertheless a spectacular team effort by

the driver and fireman and the conditions on the footplate that night must have been daunting.

These pictures, taken in April 1932, provide interesting detail for the modeller. Note the collection of fire-irons on the back of the 4–6–0's tender (previous page) and their carrying brackets: twin vertical rods on the tender front plate and the U-shaped bracket mounted on the cross-brace just in front of the water tank air vents, protruding through the coal. Finally, note the dome into which water picked up from troughs entered the tank. This tender is No.3917, of 1927.

'Royal Scot' 4–6–0 No.6104 *Scottish Borderer* in original condition and painted in pre-1928 livery, with the number on the tenderside and the LMS emblem on the cabside, leaves Euston with what the original caption describes as: 'the 10.30am excursion train for Liverpool'. The picture provides a good view of the LNWR lower-quadrant semaphore signals at this point, and note also the Ramsbottom 0–6–0ST the right.

When travel by train represented, by and large, the fastest and certainly the most comfortable method of travel within the kingdom, the introduction of new and faster trains were newsworthy events and these two pictures illustrate the amount of interest which a new, fast train could generate. Left: The Mayor of Blackpool, Alderman C.E. Tatham, uncovers a carriage nameboard to inaugurate the new 'Fylde Coast Express' on July 9 1934. Above: A highly evocative picture of the inaugural 'Fylde Coast Express', ready to leave Blackpool Central station with Stanier 'Jubilee' 4–6–0 No.5558 in charge. This locomotive, built in 1934 at Crewe, was brand new at this time and un-named. No.5558 was named *Manitoba* in 1936. It was one of a series of locomotives built with a short firebox and domeless boiler, and the 4–6–0 spent 30 years at work before being withdrawn by BR in 1964 as No.45558. Blackpool Central station closed in November 1964: this site is now a coach park.

Right: This delightful view of LNWR 4–6–0 No.2522 (LMS No.8734) illustrates a goods engine on excursion passenger work in July 1936. The original caption describes the scene as: 'Modern Transport in an ancient setting', but in some respects this is not quite correct. No.8734 was built at Crewe in 1907 and the first coach is also of LNWR origin, so the train is hardly 'modern'. It would have been possible to find a more modern steam locomotive hauling new Stanier coaches — but this would have denied us a view of a member of this class carrying the express passenger headcode of one lamp over each buffer. Note the early design of LMS upper quadrant signal, with corrugated iron arms, and the arrangement of the lower arm to enable clearer sighting by the drivers of trains approaching the photographer. Finally, this picture provides the opportunity to see an example of a bridge numberplate, No.112.

Left: Described as 'An Express Passenger Train' and dated May 2 1934, this picture illustrates an unidentified LNWR 'Claughton' 4–6–0 (as rebuilt with a large boiler) probably on the approaches to London. It is a very impressive picture of a rebuilt 'Claughton' at speed, and this engine was allocated to Shed 16 — Longsight. In 1913 the LNWR commenced the construction of a class of four-cylinder 4–6–0s which finally comprised 130 locomotives, taking their class name from the pioneer locomotive LNWR No.2222 *Sir Gilbert Claughton*. The 'Claughtons' were the mainstay of the principal West Coast express trains until the arrival of the 'Royal Scot' 4–6–0s in 1927. Once in LMS ownership, their shortcomings became more evident and the 'Claughtons', by and large were withdrawn during the mid-1930s, though the final survivor, LNWR No.42 *Princess Louise*, LMS No.6004 which lost its name in 1935, survived until 1949.

Left: LMS standard 'Compound' 4–4–0 No.1095 is seen running between two tunnels on a section of the LMS main line between Derby and Manchester on May 22 1936. In 1923 the Midland Railway owned 45 'Compounds' and the class was adopted, with slight modifications, as a post-Grouping standard design. The LMS proceeded to build a further 195 examples of these highly successful locomotives and No.1095 was constructed at Derby in 1925. It was withdrawn from service after 33 years service as BR No.41095, in 1958. On the Midland Division, the 'Compounds' worked the principal main line express services until largely displaced in the mid-1930s by the new two and three cylinder 4–6–0s of Stanier design, but even so they continued to fulfil an important role working mainly secondary services.

The MR Derby-Manchester route was not an easy one, as there were many steep gradients and tunnels. In this picture it would seem as if No.1095 has just been fired — note the black smoke — and the regulator is either closed, or only just open.

One of Stanier's new two-cylinder 4–6–0s, No.5278, with LMS Dynamometer car No.1 at speed at Elstree, in April 1937. The test was to ascertain if one of these locomotives could work a 250-ton train from London to Manchester and return (380 miles in 398 minutes running time) with a view to accelerating the Winter timetable. The 'Black 5' as this class of 4–6–0s was later known, was introduced by William Stanier and the first examples, constructed by the Vulcan Foundry, entered traffic in 1934. These engines, together with the 'first batches' of other classes, were fitted with domeless boilers and low degree superheating, but it was soon realised that this combination did not suit LMS operating conditions and later batches, including No.5278, were built with domed boilers and a separate top feed, higher degree superheating and larger fireboxes. No.5278 was built by Armstrong Whitworth in 1936 and was withdrawn as BR No.45278 in 1967. The LMS Dynamometer Car seen behind No.5278 is the former LYR vehicle which at this time carried the number 45050; prior to the carriage renumbering of 1933 it had been No.10874. Note the enlarged 'live' end of the car, which enabled the test crew to see over the tender into the cab, and also the characteristic LYR bogies. The purpose of the car and its equipment was to enable tests to be conducted whereby accurate measurements of drawbar pull and speed could be taken as part of the detailed assessment of locomotive performance. The car was marshalled immediately behind the locomotive and this enabled the test apparatus to be linked directly via the tender to the charts in the car. These charts were made by recording data onto a slowly moving roll of paper which gave a permanent record of the journey. The staff of the dynamometer car were employed on a variety of duties: one was on the footplate in order to take accurate details of boiler pressure, regulator and reversing gear positions (cut-off), whilst another member in the car was responsible for ensuring that the pen which marked onto the chart the position of junctions and stations was triggered as necessary.

47

Right: Race trains always formed an important part of the special and excursion train potential for the 'Big Four' railway companies and the Grand National, staged at Aintree, probably provided the greatest traffic potential for the LMS. Without the benefit of motorways it was a long haul from London to Liverpool by those who could afford cars and for the remainder, a train was the only alternative. In this picture, taken on March 28 1930 we see one of the Aintree 'specials' pulling out of Euston. While it is not possible to identify the pilot engine the train engine is 'Prince of Wales' 4–6–0 LMS No.5684 (LNWR No.2092) *Arabic.* Built at Crewe in 1916, *Arabic* later became LMS No.25684 when its original LMS number (5684) was required for a new three-cylinder 4–6–0 of the 'Jubilee' class. As No.25684 the engine was withdrawn from service in 1936.

Above and right: This pair of carefully posed pictures were doubtless inspired by the classic Southern Railway picture, which showed a small boy with his luggage speaking to the Southern Railway driver telling him: "I'm taking an early holiday 'cos I know summer comes soonest in the south". These similarly posed LMS scenes at Euston used the same highly successful emotive formula. Above: Photographed on May 9 1935, 11-years old William Donaldson and his 14-years old sister Catherine are pictured at Euston alongside a 'Royal Scot' 4–6–0 on what is almost the final leg of their 12,000 mile journey. They were orphans from Australia en-route to Bannockburn, Scotland where they were to live with their aunt. Arriving at Tilbury on the Orient Steam Navigation Company's liner *Orsova*, the LMS thereafter took charge for the trip to Scotland. Right: Taken on April 7 1936, this picture was captioned 'Please Mr Driver' and depicts two youngsters at Euston prior to their departure for their Easter holidays. The locomotive which was to haul their train is 4-6-0 'Royal Scot' No.6165 *The Ranger (12th London Regiment).* Built at Derby in 1930, No.6165 was converted with a Type 2A taper boiler by British Railways in 1952 and withdrawn as No.46165 in 1964.

Left: In 1939 there was a concerted effort to evacuate children away from the cities which the authorities were convinced would be attacked from the air as soon as war broke out. Accordingly, in August and September of 1939 thousands of children were moved to areas which were less likely to be the subject of mass bombing raids. However, it was natural that parents would wish to see their children and so this December 3 1939 view depicts two trains filled with London area parents and friends en route from the Capital to see children evacuated to the Northampton area. Evacuation thus provided much extra traffic for the LMS. The train engine is a class 5P/5F 4-6-0 painted in the 1936 livery style, which suggests that it is likely to be one of the number series 5225–5251, which entered traffic carrying this livery style. The coach is a Period III corridor third brake, probably built to diagram 1905.

In many respects this is a 'pure LNWR view' and since the date of the photograph was May 1923, less than five months after the Grouping, this is not, altogether surprising. In this picture we see a named, although unidentified member of the 'Prince of Wales' 4-6-0 class, piloting a double-headed special working to Blackpool, organised by match manufacturers Bryant & May. Smoke and steam make it impossible to identify the train engine, or the make up of the train, and one is left wondering if the flags will survive the journey to Blackpool and back to London again!

Right: This evocative picture, taken on September 10 1933, provides a splendid example of how the original caption writers appreciated few railway technicalities, and whilst in some cases this was unimportant, in certain cases it led to the drafting of inaccurate explanatory text. In this instance the caption writer said: "So popular has become the new prices for railway holiday travel that the LMS Lake District express is being continued for another month. So huge was the load of passengers that two engines had to be employed to draw the long train." He has actually misunderstood the role of the banker, which having drawn in the empty coaches is now giving assistance from the rear, at the beginning of the run which commenced with the taxing climb up Camden bank. In this view we see an unidentified 'Patriot' 4–6–0 heading a northbound train, though unfortunately the special train number obscures the locomotive smokebox numberplate.

Below: This very impressive photograph depicts a 4–6–0 of the 'Royal Scot' class photographed leaving Euston on September 27 1932. Unfortunately, the large headboard prevents identification of the locomotive working the train, which conveyed passengers travelling to the Hillman Company's Coventry factory for a preview of the new models which were to be launched at the forthcoming Motor Show, at Olympia. The locomotive appears to be fitted with mismatched smoke deflectors.

Above, left: An August 1937 view which shows an unidentified 'Patriot' 4–6–0 departing from Euston with a special train filled with distributors, dealers, the press and other interested persons en-route to the Hillman factory, at Coventry, to inspect the new Hillman 14 and other new season's models. While it is not possible to identify the locomotive it is possible to confirm that the coach carrying a Hillman nameboard (above, right) is Corridor Brake Third No.5574. It is an example of Lot 739, built at Wolverton in 1934 to diagram 1905 and is interesting in so far as it was a period III carriage turned out in the fully lined crimson lake livery, just before the 1934 changeover to the simpler style utilising less lining.

This view was photographed at Euston circa 1923 to illustrate a special train, booked to run from Euston to Wolverhampton and return, at the start of the journey. The fireman — who looks rather young, could he be a passed cleaner who has found himself booked onto this special working? — is adjusting the train headboard, probably for the benefit of the photographer. This headboard, specially prepared at Camden, would have been securely mounted in place before the engine left the shed but it made a better picture if this young man was photographed to show him carefully adjusting it! The engine cannot be positively identified, but it is in very clean condition and appears to be a 'George the Fifth' 4–4–0.

Right: Driver Harry Mason (left) spent his 45-years of railway service at Camden, having joined the LNWR in 1888, and this picture, taken on May 26 1933 shows Driver Mason with his fireman and guard just prior to leaving Euston with 'The Royal Scot' on his final day. His locomotive was 'Royal Scot' 4–6–0 *The London Irish Rifleman*, built by the North British Locomotive Company in 1927 and previously named *Fury*. No.6138 was rebuilt with a Type 2A taper boiler in 1944 and was eventually withdrawn by British Railways as No.46138 in 1963.

Below: This view of 'Claughton' 4–6–0 No.5971 *Croxteth* was taken on the last day of the General Strike on May 15 1926 and shows the volunteer crew receiving their instructions before departing with the 'Irish Mail'. *Croxteth*, formerly LNWR No.2511, held the distinction of being the first LNWR passenger locomotive to receive the new LMS Crimson Lake livery and this view shows that it retained the LMS lettering applied to the cabsides of early repaints, prior to the use of the LMS emblem. Note also the classification '5' in the centre of the upper cab panel.

Right: The Towcester races attracted an annual train from London which, over the Olney-Towcester section was usually worked by an 0–6–0 goods engine, and here we see Fowler '4F' No.3910 at the head of a train which comprises nine coaches, mostly of pre-Group origin, in April 1931. A number of pictures taken during the 1930s of this particular train reveal that the Midland Division of the LMS always entrusted the working to an 0–6–0 of either class 3F or 4F. Much has been written about the '4F' 0–6–0s and in truth they were not easy engines to live with. In the hands of a good crew they would perform well, but an inexperienced set of men would have a very bad time. For the record, No.3910 was built at Derby in 1920, and was withdrawn by British Railways in 1959, as No.43910.

THIS locomotive was built in 1929 as part of an ultimately unsuccessful attempt by the LMS to improve upon the thermal efficiency of the express steam locomotive. The object was to produce a locomotive comparable in size with the 'Royal Scot' 4–6–0, but equipped with an ultra-high pressure boiler of German design. Ordered by the LMS from the North British Locomotive Company, at Glasgow, the locomotive had a 'Royal Scot' 4–6–0 chassis, bogie and tender, which were paired with an ultra-high pressure boiler built by Schmidt-Herschel, sponsored by the Superheater Company. The boiler was a highly complex item containing three units generating steam at pressures of 1,400psi, 900psi and 250psi. Firebox water tubes contained distilled water in a closed circuit under 1,400psi pressure, the heat from this circuit generating steam at 900psi on a second circuit which itself held 1½

tons of water. This steam was fed direct to the inside high pressure cylinder of 11½in diameter and 26in stroke. The exhaust from this cylinder was mixed with steam at 250psi pressure, produced in the ordinary firetube portion of the barrel (located in the forward part of the boiler) and this steam was then fed to the two outside low-pressure cylinders of 18in diameter and 26in stroke. Although the tractive effort was nominally the same as a 'Royal Scot', the working weight of the engine was five tons heavier. Painted in works grey — it never carried Crimson Lake — and carrying the number 6399 the engine was named Fury, taking the name previously carried by 'Royal Scot' No.6138 (see page 52). This was an unfortunate choice of name, for on February 10 1930 a firebox superpressure tube burst whilst the 4–6–0 was undergoing trials at Carstairs. The Superheater Company's inspector was killed and the LMS fireman was

Above: No.6399 *Fury*, in works grey livery, stands in the yard at the Hyde Park works, Glasgow, of the North British Locomotive Company, in steam and ready for delivery to the LMS on February 7 1930.

seriously injured; the LMS Driver and Footplate Inspector escaped with shock and minor injuries. An enquiry was held and Fury was repaired but it never ran in revenue-earning service and in due course it arrived at Derby works where it was stored out of use, excepting a handful of trial runs made between 1931 and 1934. The locomotive was again steamed successfully, under Stanier's direction, in July 1934 but he subsequently recommended that the experiment be abandoned and that No.6399 be rebuilt as a conventional locomotive. The agreement with the Superheater Company was terminated by an LMS payment of £3,000 and No.6399 was taken to Crewe, where in 1935 it was rebuilt with a taper boiler, entering service that year as No.6170 *British Legion*.

Above: A view from inside the tender coal space, showing the cab layout, taken in the North British Locomotive Company works yard, at Glasgow.

Right: Framed in gateway of the NBL works, No.6399 *Fury* steams gently out onto LMS metals on February 7 1930, to undergo trial running. Note the fire-irons visible over the high wall — one wonders what lay behind, for no fire-irons could be that long!

Above: A broadside view of *Fury* which emphasises the small size of the standard Fowler tender.

Right: The erstwhile No.6399 *Fury* starts its new life as No.6170 *British Legion*, following rebuilding at Crewe in 1935. This picture illustrates No.6170's first revenue-earning run on November 13 1935. It had been named formally on the previous day by Earl Jellicoe, Admiral of the Fleet. No.6170's first run was a great occasion and at every stopping place members of the British Legion turned out with their flags, in salute. In this view, No.6170 pauses at Watford, en-route north. No.6170 was the only taper-boiler 'Scot' to carry crimson lake livery, or a Stanier- style cab.

Left: Elaborate ceremonies were organised by the LMS to name locomotives and these were usually carried out by civic or military dignitaries. Photographed in March 1937 at Blackpool, Mayor Alderman Ashton brandishes a bottle of champagne above the *Blackpool* nameplate carried by 'Patriot' 4–6–0 No.5524. This locomotive was nominally a rebuild of a 4–6–0 'Claughton' class locomotive and at first it carried No.5907, the number of the locomotive it replaced. Entering traffic in 1933, the engine was to have been named *Sir Frederick Harrison*, but it was renumbered and then named as seen in this picture. A number of 'Patriots' were rebuilt, being fitted with Type 2A taper boilers and double chimneys from 1946 but *Blackpool* remained in original condition until withdrawal as BR No.45524, in 1962.

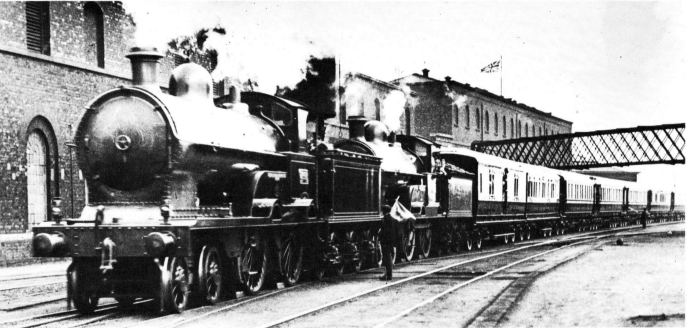

This picture depicts the LNWR Royal train, hauled by a pair of 'George the Fifth' 4–4–0s, during a visit to Crewe Works by King George V and Queen Mary, on April 21 1913. The LNWR Royal train dated from the 1900–05 period, including the emergence in 1902 of the Royal Saloons of King Edward VII and his Queen. These vehicles, as the centrepiece of the train, could be accompanied by a further six coaches, described as semi-Royal saloons which were almost equally well-appointed and were used by members of the Royal household and railway officials accompanying the King and Queen on their travels. The coaches were magnificently finished and we are fortunate that several vehicles from this train are preserved in the National Railway Museum, at York. The development of this train, at the turn of the century, resulted from King Edward VII's travels in a saloon built in 1899 for the Duke of Sutherland, who enjoyed the right to operate a private saloon on the railway system. This vehicle had been built at Wolverton to the design of C.A. Park, who was also responsible for the Royal vehicles constructed a few years later. The story is told that Edward VII's answer to the LNWR's enquiry about whether the King would like replacements for the Victorian Royal saloons was that new coaches should follow the style established by the Duke of Sutherland, and that they 'should be made as nearly like to the Royal yacht as possible.' The Royal train was always kept at Wolverton, where it was painted in the former LNWR livery of 'plum and spilt milk', more officially described as carmine lake and white. After the formation of the LMS in 1923 the King had queried the news that his train was to be painted in standard LMS crimson, and until 1939 it remained in LNWR colours. When war broke out it was decided that the striking LNWR livery would make the train too much of a target and it was painted crimson. Two replacement Royal saloons were built in 1941 and while it is believed that they were intended to afford better protection to the Royal family in the event of an air attack, they had actually been ordered prior to the war, in 1938. The aim was possibly to replace the entire Edwardian train but only the King and Queen's saloons were replaced, together with their power car.

Right: A considerable number of staff accompanied the Royal train and this included railway employees of varying grades whose duty was to look after the train generally and maintain it in perfect running order. This is Edwin Cowley, aged 64, who was presented with the MVO (Member of the Royal Victorian Order) by HM King George V during a journey from Ballater to London Euston. Mr Cowley, from Wolverton, had been a member of the Royal train staff for 27 years and when this picture was taken on October 12 1934 he had only one more month to serve before his retirement. In this view at Wolverton, he is seen cleaning one of the Royal saloons, his medal pinned proudly on his chest.

Below: Although the locomotive is carrying LNWR livery, this photograph was taken in the LMS era in July 1924 and shows the Royal train about to depart from Euston for Liverpool. The locomotive is 'Claughton' 4–6–0 *James Bishop* still carrying LNWR No.1345. Built in 1916, this engine became LMS No.5924 and was withdrawn from service in 1934 after a working life of just 18 years.

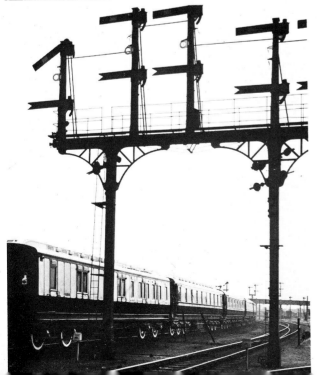

Top: On July 3 1933, brand new 'Patriot' 4–6–0 No.5996, then un-named, but which later became LMS No.5528, BR No.45528 and was named *REME* in 1960, hauls the Royal train through the LMS station at South Kenton, which was opening on the same day. The Royal travellers were en-route-from London Euston to Chatsworth, in Derbyshire.

Above: Not every journey of the Royal train conveyed passengers, and here the train is running as empty stock, but under the No.1 headcode, with one lamp over each buffer. Photographed on September 29 1934 at Rugby, the train was en-route from its base at Wolverton to Ballater, where the Royal family was staying. It was due to take the King and Queen to Glasgow for the launching of the new Cunard liner, the *RMS Queen Mary*. Hauling the train on this first leg of the journey is 'Royal Scot' 4–6–0 No.6119 *Lancashire Fusilier*, built in 1927 by the North British Locomotive Company. The locomotive is fitted with angle-topped smoke deflectors and a coal-railed tender and it is worth noting that the leading vehicle is a six-wheeled LNWR Covered Combination Truck. No.6119 was rebuilt with a Type 2A taper boiler and double-chimney in 1944, and was finally withdrawn from service as BR No.46119 in 1963.

Left: After photographing the train approaching (above) the photographer has swung round to picture the receding rear coach, an unidentified first class brake. Also of interest in this picture is the superb LNWR signal gantry: the 'D' spectacles on the three left-hand signals indicated that a plunger was located at the foot of the post, which the fireman could press to sound an audible warning in the signalbox that his train was standing at the signal.

ALTHOUGH the largest amount of LMS revenue was generated by the movement of mineral and freight traffic it was, not surprisingly, the transport of 'human freight' which produced the greatest interest from the public point of view. Indeed this 'human freight' was unique in so far that it was the only traffic carried by rail which both loaded and unloaded itself with minimal supervision at both ends of the journey! However this traffic did require certain special facilities in the form of stations, although these facilities could range from the very primitive halt to the quite grand and elaborate, as illustrated amply in the chapter dealing with Euston.

Nevertheless, regardless of the type of traffic carried, human or otherwise, all travelled under the control of the signalman who operated the fixed signals which regulated the safe movement of trains, and it is therefore with signals and signalmen that we begin this look at signals and stations, old and new.

SIGNALS & STATIONS

Right, above: Reputed to be the largest signal gantry in the British Isles, although only because all its arms were duplicated, the Rugby 'Bedstead' was far from typical of LMS or LNWR signalling practice in general terms. Construction of the London extension of the old Manchester, Sheffield & Lincolnshire Railway (later renamed the Great Central Railway) had caused some resignalling work to be undertaken at Rugby station, where the new line crossed over the LNWR. The bridge, south of Rugby, caused 'sighting problems' for LNWR drivers and the gantry, as illustrated, was built in 1895. The tall signals were intended to give a clear and early sight while the lower arms repeated the aspect for close sighting and were additionally useful in foggy weather! The left hand group of three posts applied to trains on the down main line from Blisworth and controlled: To Goods; To Down Through; To Platform. The central group of five posts applied to the down line from Northampton and controlled: To Goods; To Down Through; To Platform; To Bay; To Bay. Finally, the right hand group of five posts applied to up trains from Market Harborough and controlled: To Goods; To Down Through; To Platform; To Bay; To Bay.

The LMS resignalled the Rugby area in 1939 by replacing the existing semaphores with colour lights and the famous gantry became redundant. However, when this picture was taken on December 19 1934 these changes were still a few years away. In this view we see every signal set at danger with 'Prince of Wales' class 4–6–0 No.25673 *Lusitania* blowing off from the safety valves while waiting for a clear road. Built as LNWR No.1100 in 1916, it became LMS No.5673 and in the year of this

photograph had 20000 added to its number in order to release No.5673 for a new class 5XP 4–6–0 which was to be built. *Lusitania* was one of the final survivors of its class, being withdrawn in January 1949. BR number 58001 was allocated but it was not actually carried by the engine. For the record, the last of the 'Princes' was LMS No.25752 (originally LNWR No.1357) dating from 1919, which was never named.

Above: In May 1926, 70-years-old volunteer signalman Thomas Towener is at work during the General Strike in what the original caption describes as 'the main signalbox at Euston'. Volunteers did much to help keep the trains moving during this difficult period. A posed shot, this scene nevertheless illustrates the cloth, or duster, which was held in the hand which pulled over the lever after the catch had been released. Note the LNWR practice of not mounting the signal and other repeaters on a block instrument shelf which ran the length of the frame. The short shelf in this view houses only the block instruments; the signal repeaters are visible on the low-level pedestal behind the lever-frame.

Below, left: Taken at Ambergate Station Junction on May 22 1936, this picture illustrates the interior of a Midland Railway signal box, with the instruments mounted at eye-level and located as near as possible over the levers to which they refer. The unusual triangular station layout permitted trains travelling north from Derby to go to either Chesterfield via Clay Cross, or Manchester via the High Peak. In addition, it permitted trains to leave the Chesterfield line and take the Manchester route without reversing. In the platform, '483 Class' 4—4—0 No.337 is in charge of a stopping train bound for Derby. No.337 became BR No.40337, and was withdrawn from service in 1958.

Below, right: Although photographed in Liverpool Lime Street out of the LMS period, in 1954, this view of a more modern power box miniature lever-frame provides an interesting contrast with the manual signalbox interiors.

Right: St Pancras (opened in 1868) in all its splendour, viewed from the west — with King's Cross station just visible in the distance. Note the imposing cast-iron gates, removed after 1893 when Somers Town Goods depot was opened. Much has been written about St Pancras station, and certainly no other London station, or any of its provincial counterparts, aroused such controversy as the Midland Railway's terminus in the Capital. The debate began with the eviction of the previous occupants of the site, continued with the treatment of the St Pancras churchyard and complaints by shareholders about the enormous cost of the structure, and has persisted to more recent times as a result of proposals to close the station.

However the greatest argument, and one which continues to this day, concerns the architectural style of the building and in particular, the hotel, opened in May 1873. The entire argument was based on style and taste, and designer Scott was the subject of lengthy abuse before the structure was completed. Described as 'showy and expensive' St Pancras was seen as a striking contrast to its neighbour, the Great Northern Railway's Kings Cross terminus, which was held to be 'simple, characteristic and true'. However, not everyone was critical about St Pancras. 'The Times', when architect Scott died, said: "St Pancras was the most beautiful terminus in London." Other writers have described it: "the noblest of all the structures of this kind in London," and "it stands without rival for palatial beauty, comfort and convenience." St Pancras is now a listed building and has been fully cleaned. So much for the emotions aroused by St Pancras, why was it such a catalyst of reaction? Was it the capacious train shed, with its superb frontal block, backing onto a 245ft single span

overall station roof, which at that time was the largest of its kind in the world? Perhaps it was the beer cellar, which featured 720 cast-iron columns upon which the station floor stood. Indeed, the station itself is on 'the first floor', while the beer cellar was in reality the 'ground floor'. Perhaps it was the fact that these columns were so spaced as to provide the maximum storage space for the beer barrels. The essence of St Pancras was the traffic conveyed, and in 1922 the statistics were: number of passengers booked — 1,028,010; number of season tickets issued — 2,534; total coaching receipts—£872,599; working expenses £54,781.

Right, above: A view of St Pancras from the east, circa 1880. The original design for the terminus would have produced an even more imposing structure, as Scott had intended to give the building five floors. However, rising costs prompted the MR Board of Directors to order that the station and hotel should be built with only four floors.

Right: An impressive interior view of St Pancras, circa 1912. The tank engine to the right appears to be an 0–4–4T of Kirtley design, a class long associated with the station. The non-passenger stock in the centre is a mixed selection in which the open carriage trucks can be clearly seen. Note the twin gas pipes on the carriage roof, for until 1908 a single pipe was more usual. The second pipe was added to allow the provision of pilot lights.

Right: An attractive study of the exterior of Liverpool's Lime Street station, which was described by the original caption as one of "England's gloomy railway stations." It continued "The unsightly and ugly approach to Lime Street station, which is notorious in the fact that it is considered to have a particularly ugly and dreary interior!" The picture was taken on October 8 1929.

Left: Although this study of Liverpool Lime Street, the work of 'Picture Post' photographer Bert Hardy, was taken slightly outside the 'Big Four' era, in 1954, it is highly evocative of the LMS period. Steam from the safety valves of a Stanier 4–6–0 — possibly a 'Black 5' — is roaring into the station roof, the fireman is watching for the guard's 'rightaway' while a young railwayman passes the engine, attending to the oil lamps. On the right of the picture a young trainspotter, wearing his school cap, sits on a platform trolley awaiting the next arrival.

Left: Taken at Wembley & Sudbury in March 1925 this photograph proves that the marking of platform edges with white lines was not a wartime practice introduced between 1939 and 1945 to help passengers combat problems of travel during the blackout — a theory which has previously appeared in print.

Below: The Midland Railway station at Leicester, in 1925. Built in 1892, the station changed little during the LMS period.

Facing page, top: Brand new Vulcan Foundry-built LMS Standard 'Compound' 4–4–0 No.918 heads an up express at Gleneagles, in 1927. Gleneagles was world famous for its hotel and golf course, and this picture illustrates the unusual station building arrangements. No.918, later British Railways No.40918, survived until withdrawal in 1952, when six standard 'Compound' 4–4–0s were withdrawn, the first of the class to be taken out of service.

Facing page, lower: The majority of stations operating on the LMS network from 1923 to 1948 were those which the Company had inherited but some new ones were built, as at Apsley, Hertfordshire. Located south of Hemel Hempstead and Boxmoor, its prime purpose was to serve the growing residential population and to provide a convenient station for the 5,000 employees of papermakers John Dickinson and Company, whose factory stood very close to the railway. A spectacular opening ceremony was staged with Stanier 2–6–4T No.2446 crashing through a paper banner, appropriately enough provided by the Dickinson factory. The opening ceremony was performed jointly by LMS Chairman Lord Stamp and Dickinson Chairman Sir Reginald Benson, on September 22 1938. It is worth noting that No.2446, carrying express passenger train lights, had worked a special train conveying officials from London. However these Western Division 2–6–4Ts allocated to the London area were more normally employed on passenger work between Euston and Bletchley, although at times other 'outer destinations', such as Tring, marked the end of the northbound terms of duty.

Right: After the fall of France in 1940 Britain waited anxiously for German parachute troops to arrive in an attempt to conquer the country. One defence was to try to ensure that any invading Germans would not know where they were, and in this picture we see LMS painters at work obliterating the name of Bushey & Oxhey station. This practice probably caused untold problems for those who were trying to defend the country, but it was typical of some of the extreme measures taken by the authorities during the frantic months when we stood alone in World War II.

Above: The busiest suburban line on the LMS system was the LT&S section in Essex, and under construction here is a new station at Gale Street, between Barking and Dagenham, provided to serve a new housing estate at Becontree. Photographed in June 1926 is LTSR 4–4–2T No.2178, carrying a Fenchurch Street destination board at the head of a train comprised almost entirely of LTSR stock. The exception is the second vehicle, a Period I LMS third class non-corridor brake. No.2178 was originally LTSR No.81 *Aveley*, built by Robert Stephenson in 1909. This engine became MR No.2178 in 1912 and lost its name. By 1929 it had been renumbered 2149 and following nationalisation it became BR No.41967. The locomotive, withdrawn in 1952, was one of the final four 4–4–2Ts built during LTSR ownership. They were the largest 4–4–2Ts owned by this company and it is fortunate that LTSR No.80 *Thundersley* is preserved. Note the North London Railway poster-board on the far platform.

Right: As the London suburbs expanded, new stations were built to serve the needs of the growing resident population and an LNWR electric unit enters the station under construction at South Kenton, between Harrow & Wealdstone and Wembley on the London to Watford line. Opened on July 3 1933, the station buildings were constructed of enamelled steel sheet, mounted onto a wooden framework.

Left: The timber-and-slate station room and booking office at Gale Street (see also opposite page, below) was far from being a grand affair, but this picture reveals a wealth of detail for the railway modeller. Included as 'Gale Street Halt' in the 1926 LMS timetable, the station was renamed Becontree on July 18 1932.

Below: The view looking west from the footbridge at Gale Street, as Midland Railway 0–6–0 No.3306 approaches with a stopping passenger train in June 1926. While the LT&S was normally the preserve of tank engines, initially of the 4–4–2T type, and then later of the 2–6–4T variety, tender locomotives were not unknown and included 2–4–0 and 4–4–0 types together with a variety of 0–6–0 goods engines. No.3306 was built by Kitson as Midland Railway No.2029 in 1891, and was renumbered 3306 in 1907. The engine was rebuilt with a Type G7 boiler (as illustrated here) in 1920, and it survived until 1960 when British Railways withdrew it from service as No.43306.

Left: Another new station opened in 1933 on the LT&S section was Chalkwell, between Westcliffe-on-Sea and Leigh-on-Sea. Compared with Gale Street (see above) this was a rather more imposing brick-built structure. The poster boards carry LMS lettering in black on a yellow background, rather than the usual white letters and black background. Once again, much interesting detail , especially for the modeller.

Left: Still on the LT&S section, this is the imposing exterior of Tilbury Riverside Station, photographed on January 25 1933 from the landing stage. This station, opened on May 16 1930, replaced Tilbury Marine, which closed on May 1 1932.

WE conclude this series of photographs looking at LMS stations by depicting two 'High Street' passenger facilities provided by the LMS. They provide ample illustration of the fact that there was far more to railways than just trains:

Right, above: This stylish parcels and goods receiving office in Cannon Street, London, was brand new when this publicity photograph was taken on April 10 1931. In the window are displayed a selection of LMS booklets, timetables and pamphlets, while the poster on the left, headed 'April', lists excursions operating from Euston and St Pancras. Even the letterbox flap (just below the left-hand corner of the window) is proudly inscribed 'LMS', whilst the elegant lettering above the shop leaves the passing public in no doubt as to which was Britain's premier railway system! These 'shops' were known as 'town offices.'

Right, below: The LMS enquiry kiosk and seat reservation office at Rhyl station. The photograph was taken in sunny weather on June 8 1939, but the happy days of rail travel and holidays were soon to end, when the outbreak of World War II on September 3 1939 rapidly changed the life and travelling habits of the British people.

GOODS
AND
MINERAL TRAFFIC

IT WAS not the glamorous passenger trains which generated the bulk of the LMS Railway Company's revenue; the biggest business was in goods and mineral traffic, predominantly coal. If we take the last full year before the outbreak of World War II, we find that while passenger train receipts totalled £18,884,955, general merchandise traffic receipts were £17,224,043, while minerals totalled £18,738,601. Add to this a further £523,019 for livestock and we have receipts from 'goods train traffic' totalling £36,485,663 — almost twice as much money as the passenger traffic produced.

Thus, immediate pre World War II traffic levels were rather lower than the equivalent figures for 1929, when passenger train receipts were £19,306,470 while the total 'Goods train figures' were £43,816,074. In fact, during the 1930s the LMS never did recover sufficiently to match the revenue figures for 1929, but with the advent of the World War II statistics

became less meaningful.

If we examine the facts behind the figures we find that in 1938 the LMS conveyed 124,089,593 tons of 'Goods train traffic', comprising 25,973,566 tons of general merchandise with the remainder in the various mineral classes. Within this total, 63.81% of general goods and 81.22% of the mineral traffic originated on the LMS system.

The livestock figures have to be calculated in Equated Tonnage and this figure totalled 835,023 tons, which in itself is a large amount. Surprisingly the largest single category was sheep, followed by cattle and pigs. In fact the figure for sheep was more than double the cattle tonnage which was almost double the figure for pigs.

All this traffic was conveyed in a mixture of railway-owned (not all LMS) and privately-owned vehicles and the division was almost 50/50. If one takes the statistics for the week ending March 23 1935, the exact percentages are: 49.75% carried in

railway-owned wagons and 50.25% in privately-owned wagons, with the privately-owned wagons generating 50.98% of the receipts.

One could ask how far all the traffic was hauled, and taking the same week in 1935, we find that the Company average for 'Land sale coal traffic' was 35.69 miles in railway company vehicles, while those vehicles belonging to the private owners managed to achieve 49.52 miles.

Combining the statistics for the whole wagon fleet produces some very large figures and in 1935 the Company's total wagon mileage was 1,884,369,275. Examination of this total reveals that merchandise and livestock accounted for 787,738,859 miles while mineral traffic mileage was 502,092,651. To this loaded total must be added empty wagon miles which reached the staggering figure of 594,537,765 in 1935. If we look at the distances the wagons travelled then we discover that the overall average was 49.14 miles.

Left: In order to set this business into perspective, we commence this review of LMS goods traffic, as seen by the media of the day, with this magnificent view of a yard full of wagons loaded with many different grades of coal. The date is February 1940 and while the location was not recorded (because of the war) it appears to be Cricklewood. In the centre background is an LMS standard class 3F 0–6–0T. What makes this view most interesting is the profusion of coal wagons, almost all privately owned and all generally in very good condition. However, six years of wartime neglect took its toll and by 1945 much of the wagon fleet was in poor condition.

Right: Although this photograph was taken just before the LMS was formed, its inclusion is justified in that little changed during the next few years, other than the company ownership markings on the wagons. The picture depicts the MR yard at Bradford in July 1921. Probably the most interesting vehicle is the MR meat van on the extreme left: some of these vans (built to diagram 379) were converted to carry banana traffic, but this vehicle does not show any evidence of this change of use. The four wagons and van on the siding next to the meat van are of Great Central, Lancashire & Yorkshire, Midland, Caledonian and Glasgow & South Western Railway ownership which reflects the effects of the common-user policy introduced during World War I to reduce empty wagon mileage. The group of four vehicles (three wagons and one van) in the top left of the picture include examples owned by the GSWR and LNWR. Apart from the LNWR van against the stop block in the centre of the picture, it is difficult to positively identify other vehicles, however the van on the right of the picture has a sliding roof-door. Finally, it is worth noting the number of loaded open goods wagons sheeted over, and the proportion of motor lorries (three), to horse drawn vehicles (five).

Above: Milk was an important commodity which travelled by rail and this May 1925 picture, depicting the North Staffordshire lines at Uttoxeter, underlines this point. Although this was two years after the Grouping, the van is still carrying its LNWR livery and running number. Milk churns remained in use for another 20 years, but in the early 1930s the milk tank wagon appeared and this method gradually rendered the milk churn obsolete.

Right: This is a fascinating picture from September 1941 and judging by the original caption it is evident that the LMS was very proud that mobile teams of rat catchers like this were very effective. Indeed, the company proudly boasted that the destruction of goods stored on its property was kept down to an absolute minimum! Jim Fortey and Alfred Greenwin were responsible for the line between Southend and Wellingborough, presumably only the Midland Division and LTS Section. In addition to their dogs they also carried ferrets in the boxes slung over their shoulders. They were based in the London area presumably.

Above: During the 1930s competition from road transport together with the need to improve handling methods led to some new innovations and in 1938 the LMS produced eight six-wheeled chassis (to Diagram 1988) each capable of carrying two insulated and electrically-heated road tank trailers. The chassis, numbered 707000–707007, were constructed at the Derby carriage and wagon works and were designed to convey edible oils between the refineries and factories used in margarine manufacture by Lever Bros. The tanks were described as being Dyson Road Rail trailers, and these two March 1938 pictures illustrate them being displayed to interested parties and the press at Euston, where they were reversed onto their carrying wagon by a three-wheeled 'mechanical horse.'

Probably the most important single goods traffic development between the wars was the container. While it was not a new idea, (containers of sorts had been used for many years) it was probably the Grouping of 1923 which led to a rationalisation of facilities which accelerated the development of the railborne container. The first 100K type containers were built at Earlestown in 1932 and had a carrying capacity of three tons, and a 650 cu. ft. capacity. Their nominal weight was 1 ton 9cwt 2qtrs and livery was crimson lake with yellow lettering. In this picture we see K151 (left) and K66 (right) LMS containers at Olympia on August 26 1934.

Right: One of the fascinating points to emerge from the study of the original captions are the technical inaccuracies evident in some instances. This group of delegates from 'Empire Parliaments' is described as viewing at Euston an example of a new type of freight carrying vehicle and confirms that the example under examination is for carrying glass. What the writer probably did not realise is that glass carrying wagons had been in use for many years prior to July 25 1935, when this picture was taken. Perhaps it was a 'slow' news day? Large panes of glass were stood vertically in the well of the wagon, held firmly by the screw clamps on the upright struts.

Left: An important development during the late 1930s was the shock-absorbing wagon. This picture depicts prototype wagon No.450000 being demonstrated to the press on August 17 1937. Several months elapsed before any further examples were constructed but in total a further 699 wagons were built by the LMS, with the final examples entering traffic after Nationalisation. The demonstration to the press took place at St Pancras Goods Depot (Somers Town) and was intended to show that the damage resulting from heavy impact during shunting could be considerably reduced. This picture shows one of the technicians adjusting the instrument which recorded impact shock.

Below: MR 0–6–0T No.1660 prepares to demonstrate the shock-absorbing wagon, which is carrying a group of observers who clearly aim to experience the impact-test at first hand! The shock-absorbing equipment is visible on the sole bar. No.1660 was built in 1878 as MR No.1377, and survived until withdrawal in 1953 as BR No.41660. This was doubtless a serious scientific experiment, but this picture has a distinct comic aspect!

It was naturally the spectacular rather than the ordinary which attracted press attention and this shipment of a consignment of Works of Art from Paris, for exhibition at the Royal Academy, is a good example. Above: On December 8 1931 LMS 0–6–2T No.2232 hauls two vehicles carrying crates which are sheeted over to provide extra protection. The location is the Commercial Road Depot, and the police guard is an indication of the value of the consignment. No.2232 was built in 1912 and was allocated LTSR No.85; however by the time the locomotive entered traffic the LTSR had been purchased by the Midland Railway and it became MR No.2192. The LMS renumbered it 2232 but in 1939 it reverted back to its old number, 2192. It was renumbered yet again, becoming No.1992 when No.2192 was required for a new 2–6–4T. It finally became British Railways No.41992, and was withdrawn from service in 1959.

The bogie wagon design (below) is particularly interesting and while the official designation was '35-ton machinery trolley', these vehicles were also known as 'Rectanks'. They were built to Government order in World War I to carry army tanks and then after the war they were sold to the railway companies, those going to the old Midland Railway Company being adapted to carry two wooden bolsters, which can be clearly seen on the trolley nearest the camera. However, this vehicle is carrying an LMS numberplate, so it cannot accurately be stated when it was taken into LMS stock: if it was a former MR vehicle one would expect it to still be fitted with a Midland plate, as this company's stock retained their numbers into the LMS period.

Above, left: The export of large railway locomotives was a regular feature in the LMS period and their shipment naturally attracted press attention. When it came to locomotive building, Britain was still the 'workshop of the world'. A pair of 'Pacific' locomotives (Nos.2654 and 2656) are pictured prior to loading aboard ship, and while their destination is the North West Railway in India, their origin is clearly the Vulcan Foundry, at Newton-le-Willows. Note the especially-long towing shackle, and the hefty 'U-bolts' secured into the lifting-holes in the main frames just ahead of the smokebox.

Above, right: On February 19 1930, 4–6–2 No.2655, bound for India's North West Railway, is lowered carefully into the hold of the *SS Belpamela* at Gladstone Docks, Liverpool, following transfer by rail by the LMS from the Vulcan Foundry, Newton-le-Willows. The locomotive, one of a batch of 16, weighed 90 tons. One of the batch of nine tenders also shipped to India with the 4–6–2s is just visible standing on the dock on the left. The *Belpamela* was the same ship used to transport No.6220 *Coronation* and its train across the Atlantic Ocean, in 1939. (See pages 35–36).

Above: LMS class 3F 0–6–0T No.16687 shunts two Nasmyth-built 2–8–2 locomotives, during shipment to China. This picture emphasises the large bulk of these China-bound engines, which 'dwarf' shunting locomotive No.16687, built in 1928 by Beardmore. Following the 1934 renumbering scheme, designed to place all standard locomotives within the number series 1–9999, this engine became No.7604. A genuine shunting locomotive No.16687, unlike many of the series, was fitted only with a locomotive steam brake and as such did not carry train end pipes (vacuum pipes); therefore it was unable to haul passenger trains. As British Railways No.47604 it survived until 1962. Painted on the end of the four-wheeled tank wagon on the right is the wording: '207 Redline-Clico Super-Petrol'.

Right: A Nasmyth 2–8–2 is loaded aboard the *SS Belpamela*, which on this occasion was bound for China with its motive power cargo, on December 14 1932. The locomotive was one of a batch of eight 2–8–2s, originally numbered 291–8, later renumbered 1594–1601. According to the contemporary caption, the transfer of this locomotive by rail to the docks required the LMS to slew its tracks through one station, and lower the metals under three bridges in order to give the necessary clearance.

AS might be expected, the news photographers of these years were most interested in the big, bulky loads which provided headaches for the operating staff of the LMS. The following five pictures provide examples of the type of goods traffic which originally went by rail, but which now regrettably causes much congestion on our roads.

Left: On December 3 1926, a new bronze propeller for the Cunard liner *RMS Mauretania* is loaded at Camden, prior to despatch to Liverpool, on what appears to be an LNWR 'Weltrolley'.

Below: A 12ft diameter condenser, weighing 10 tons, is pictured following its arrival at Stonebridge Park (LMS) station power house, which supplied the power to the electrified line from Euston to Watford. It appears to be loaded onto a 25-ton standard LMS four-wheel trolley to Special Wagon diagram book page 106.

Centre, left: Here we see an example of what the original caption writer described as 'an old type London bus' which, having been withdrawn from service, was being sent to Chesterfield for breaking-up. Photographed at St Pancras Goods depot on May 26 1937, the bus is being placed upon a Midland Railway bogie tramcar truck (to Midland Railway diagram 318), classified by the LMS as a 15-ton bogie tramcar truck (Skeleton). The vehicle appeared on page 64 of the LMS Special Wagon Diagram book. Built in 1904/5, nine examples were in service, until circa 1950.

Above: In this picture we see sections, each weighing between 15 and 23 tons, of a giant rotary crane constructed by Vickers at Barrow in Furness. Photographed in July 1926, the load is being conveyed on a variety of bogie 'Weltrolleys.'

Right: This November 1934 picture affords an impressive view of an LMS transformer truck in traffic. The vehicle is apparently one of a pair of 80-ton vehicles built in 1926; No.17000 (of Lot 245) and No.327 (of Lot 340). Both vehicles were allocated to page 136 in the LMS Special Wagon Diagram Book. The large electric transformer which formed the load was conveyed from Manchester to Harlesden and is seen here alongside a signal box of Midland Railway origin. The shunter (or guard, it is not clear which) is handing a document to the signalman, perhaps a wrong line order. It should be remembered that these publicity pictures frequently placed railwaymen in unusual situations simply to make what the press photographer thought would be a good picture. Whatever the circumstances this view does provide a splendid picture of a bulky load and a useful close-up study of a Midland Railway signal box.

Facing page, lower: A very interesting view of the bogie shop at Wolverton, in 1911. Whilst this picture is one of a series which depicts carriage building at Wolverton in the pre-Grouping era, its inclusion is valid in that little changed in methods of carriage construction, at least during the early years of LMS operations.

Above: A carriage takes shape in the body-building shop at Wolverton. The basic framework is complete and construction of the roof will follow.

WOLVERTON WORKS
AND
LMS COACHES

WITH the formation of the LMS in 1923, the new Company inherited a number of workshops which built locomotives, carriages and wagons, but in the realm of the passenger carrying coach, only three workshops, at Derby (ex-Midland Railway), Newton Heath, (ex-Lancashire & Yorkshire Railway) and Wolverton (ex-London & North Western Railway) actually continued to build new coaches for the new company.

Unlike locomotives, which saw the imposition of Midland Railway standards and the construction of existing, albeit modified, Midland Railway designs it was not to be a total Midland Railway takeover in this area of passenger carrying vehicles. The new LMS management was persuaded to adopt LNWR carriage dimensions and interior arrangements for general service stock and to build its early sleep-

ing and dining cars to a design which owed much to LNWR style. However, the stock was to be painted in the Midland colour of Crimson Lake and although completion of this task occupied several years, outwardly at least it did appear as if the Midland Railway had taken over entirely.

In examining this subject we are fortunate in that a photographer visited Wolverton in 1911 and although this date was prior to the general period covered by this book, his photographs are worthy of inclusion if only because very little changed in carriage construction methods between 1911 and 1923, when Wolverton became part of the LMS.

The origins of Wolverton Works, go back to the opening of the London & Birmingham Railway (see pages 5–7) when it was the principal works of the Railway, and in 1845 Wolverton

manufactured its first locomotives, two Bury-designed 2–2–0s. In July 1846, the Manchester & Birmingham, Grand Junction and the London & Birmingham Railways came together to form the London & North Western Railway, though it should be noted that the Liverpool & Manchester had been absorbed by the Grand Junction in the previous year. Following this event, 'Wolverton Works' which had been known as 'Wolverton Station', changed its name and was now to be called 'the 'L&NWR Engine works Wolverton'. Locomotive construction and repair was to be a special feature of the works until 1877, when it ceased.

During the years that followed Wolverton Works grew steadily. As part of the LNWR policy of making everything 'in house' the works became responsible for constructing and producing a variety of products. Within the area was a gasworks which supplied all the station gas from Euston to Stafford in addition to supplying the people living in Wolverton, Old Wolverton and Stantonbury. This gasworks was to remain in railway ownership until 1955 when it was taken over by the Gas Board prior to complete closure 15 years later. Wolverton had its own iron and brass foundries, it constructed road vehicles and it even made the paint used in the repair of existing stock and construction of new vehicles.

In 1900 the power-house was built, and by the following year it was fully operational, thus making Wolverton the first railway works in the UK to be completely powered by electricity. By the Grouping, the works covered an area of 80 acres of which 37 acres were occupied by workshops and offices and it was the largest carriage building and repair works in the kingdom. It became known as the 'LMSR Carriage and Wagon Works, Wolver-

ton' — wagon building being introduced at this time.

Although R. W. Reid, the former Carriage Superintendent of the Midland Railway became Carriage Superintendent of the LMS he nevertheless adopted certain LNWR design elements into the new LMS standard coaches which in addition to the Wolverton length of 57ft. was added, the Wolverton train lighting system, and elements of the Wolverton four wheel bogie, which although similar to the Midland design, retained entirely the best LNWR design feature, namely the bolster suspension angle, and the Wolverton six wheel bogie. In essence, the new LMS standard coaches were influenced by Wolverton in respect of overall length and interior layout, and by the Midland

Railway for detail features and panel design.

The introduction of wagon building to the works required a degree of reorganisation and it should be noted that whereas the LMS was still building wooden solebar stock at Derby and elsewhere, all Wolverton's production was on steel-channel underframes, generally 17ft. 6in. long. In the years that followed Wolverton Works pro-

Above, left: A roughly hewn well-seasoned log being sawn into planks at Wolverton, for use in carriage construction. The machine tool carries the inscription 'T. Robinson & Son Ltd, Rochdale, England.'

Above, right: Insulation, as provided by thick layers of felt, is placed in position on the coach floor.

It would appear that French polishing at Wolverton was done by women — there are no men to be seen here. While ornate seat-ends dominate the shop, other items such as decorative compartment pictures and interior doors are also awaiting attention.

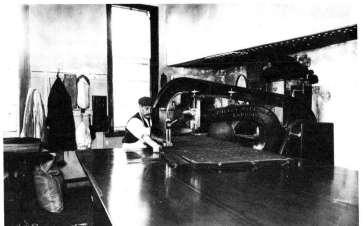

Left: The upholstery department hard at work. Seat backs and ends, of both leather and fabric, are being stuffed with horse hair and 'buttoned down' to produce the finished item.

Below: Window roller-blinds were an important feature of carriages of this period, and here we see four more neatly-attired gentlemen, all wearing immaculate shirts and ties, turning these items out by the dozen. Note the electric lighting.

Above: A works operator is cutting cloth required for seat manufacture, using a powered cutter which carries the inscription 'Aublet Harry & Co, London'.

Right: Using a lathe driven by a flat belt turned by an overhead lineshaft, this man is machining a carriage axle. Note the piles of 'swarf' produced by the lathe, and the large pile of finished axles, ready to be fitted to their wheels. The belt powering the tools from the overhead shaft would have to be protected by wire mesh guards today, to prevent accidents.

duced a vast array of LMS freight stock which ran on both split and solid spoked wheels, although later the solid wheel centre became standard. In addition, the works produced Mansell wheels, first introduced in 1848 with the final batch being manufactured in 1936. These distinctive wheels, with the oak (or teak) centre and cast-iron boss, retaining ring and central plate are clearly illustrated in this chapter.

LMS carriage construction began with the standard coach, which comprised a wooden framed and panelled, high-waisted vehicle, fully beaded on the outside with a wood and canvas roof. Corridor coaches had a full complement of outer doors and this design style is now generally referred to as 'Period One'. The second style, referred to as 'Period Two' began in 1929 with the abandonment of outside compartment doors on corridor coaches and the introduction of larger windows with slightly rounded corners. During this period steel panelling was introduced and beading was abandoned.

Following the appointment of William Stanier in 1932 a third design style was introduced and this style, generally referred to as 'Period Three', saw the arrival of the completely flush-sided steel coach, with well rounded window corners and this design style with slight modifications was to remain the LMS standard for the remainder of the Company's existence.

Right: Steel tyres for wheels were heated to expand them sufficiently to lower them over the wheel, after which they were shrunk into position, a task being undertaken in this picture.

Left: An interesting comparison of wheel construction. On the right is a set of Mansell wheels, which have a cast-iron boss, oak (or teak) segments, cast-iron retaining ring and steel tyre. On the left is a more modern all-steel set of wheels. Wooden wheels were built until the 1930s.

Right: A detailed photograph of a pair of wheels being profiled on a wheel lathe. The template lying in line with the wheel tread was used by the operator from time to time to check the flange profile, while the four large bolts secured the cutting tool in position.

Right: An overhead travelling crane built by Craven Brothers of Manchester, in 1899, lowers a completed carriage underframe onto a newly-constructed pair of bogies. The underframe is being carefully aligned as it descends by men at each end, holding ropes tied to the buffers.

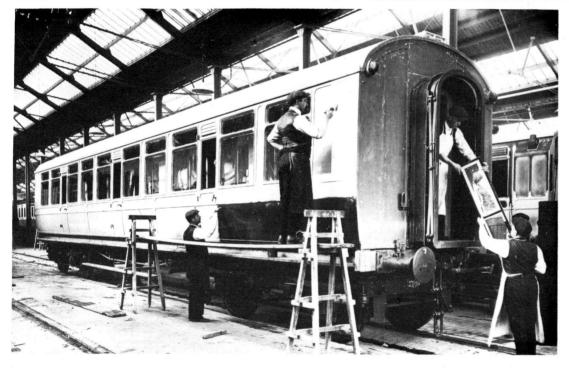

Left, above: A carriage nears completion. A pair of painters are busy on the outside of this vehicle, whilst two men are fitting out the interior — decorative framed prints are just being taken inside, to adorn compartment walls. This un-numbered corridor coach was probably built to diagram D 267. This final style of elliptically-roofed stock first appeared in 1907, but in 1911 there was a change in body styling, when toplights were introduced.

Left, below: LNWR No.1570, believed to be an all-third class 50ft elliptical roof toplight, built to D 267, emerges from the paintshop No.2 road at Wolverton, ready for service in immaculate 'plum and spilt milk' livery.

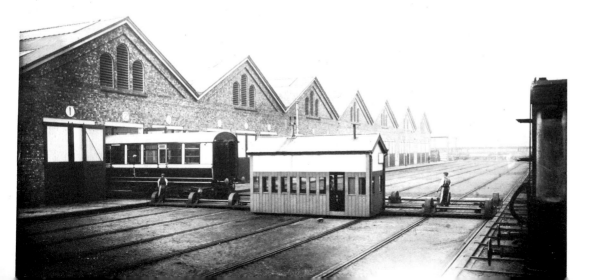

Right: During 1925/26 a number of all-steel coaches were built for the LMS by outside contractors, possibly paid for with low interest Government loans as part of an attempt to assist the steel industry. This view, at Euston, of third class vestibule coach No.6034 (later No.8039) of Lot 185, built by the Metropolitan Carriage, Wagon and Finance Co. shows an example of a carriage built to Diagram D 1745. Although built with a flush sided exterior, this stock was lined out in the full livery, a style normally associated with panelled, beaded stock.

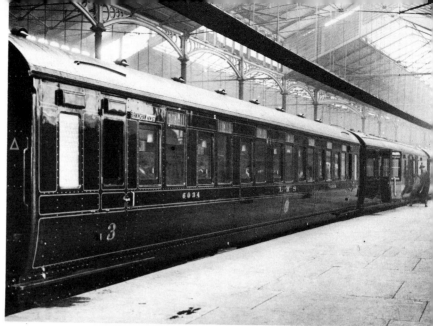

Below: 'Claughton' 4–6–0 No.162 storms up the bank from Euston on April 15 1926 with a special train of all-steel carriages (see above) comprising D 1745 third class vestibule and D 1746 brake third stock. This was a special train, running from Euston to Birmingham with the purpose of displaying the new stock to the press and other interested parties. No.162 was built in 1917 and was never named. It was withdrawn as LMS No.5933 at the end of 1932.

Right: Third class sleeping car No.14229, depicted at Euston at the time that these vehicles were introduced to the British railway system, in 1928. Between 1928 and 1931 85 of these coaches were built at Derby, to diagram D 1709, in four batches. Based on a 60ft underframe, the coaches had symmetrical end-to-end layout with seven compartments. None of the D 1709 stock carried the words 'Sleeping Car' on the bodysides as the coaches were convertible for day use.

Above, left: An interior view of one of the third class sleeping compartments, from the corridor. The upholstery was in fawn velvet, with mahogany trim and grey mohair carpet on the compartment floors. For day use the compartments provided four-a-side seating, the lower berth being prepared for sleeping by pulling it out from the wall slightly. The top berth was hinged to the wall, the mahogany-panelled underside giving a neat finish when it was folded away, for day use. The four berths were provided with pillows and blanket only and access to the upper berth was by a combined fold-away table and ladder. Compartments were lit by a dim blue light, automatically switched on as the main lights went out and the sleeping berth charge was six shillings per passenger. The initial 75 sleeping cars built to this design were fully beaded, with a high waist, and matchboard ends (Period 1 style); the final 10 were built using flush steel panelling. However, they retained the high waist of the original design and were fully lined. Many of these cars were modified as fixed berth cars in the 1930s, and 40 were further converted for use as ambulance vehicles during the war. After Nationalisation in 1948 17 of these vehicles were converted yet again as cafeteria and buffet cars, the remainder reverting to their original use as sleeping cars, some as convertible vehicles.

Above, right: It was not until 1935 that passengers on first class sleeping cars received the comfort of a hot water bottle and in this picture, taken on January 1 that year, a sleeping car attendant of the Euston-Inverness sleeping car train places water bottles in the compartments.

Above: The LMS did not seem particularly enamoured with the buffet car idea and only ever built five of the type. The first, illustrated here, (Car No.100) was built to D 1848 externally, to Period II styling. Four years later, in 1936, four similar vehicles to Period III styling entered traffic. In this picture we see Sir Josiah Stamp, Chairman of the LMS (second right), sampling a snack meal on June 2 1932.

Right: A LNWR Arc-roof brake third vehicle converted as pictured here for use as a Film Unit carriage, toured the LMS system and is shown being loaded ready to leave Euston station on October 8 1934, at the start of the tour. The programme of films was presented to company employees under the slogan 'See Your Own Railway On The Screen', but a wider audience was sought, and employees' relatives and friends, and customers of the Company were encouraged to attend showings. More than 2,000 people saw the films at Euston and in four performances at Crewe the figure exceeded 4,000, and similar audiences were achieved elsewhere. The Film Unit carriage carried the equipment, films and two support staff to the various venues, where use was made of local halls capable of accommodating sizeable audiences. The success of this method of 'educating' the staff led to the production of films of a specialised character dealing with particular types of railway work.

Left: The use of old passenger stock as camping coaches was part of the LMS scene and in this picture, taken at Derby on February 23 1937 we see three Midland Railway carriages and one Lancashire & Yorkshire Railway vehicle being prepared for the coming season. Note the teapots, cutlery and crockery on the table in the foreground and the deck chairs, leaning against the carriage. Although their use was comparatively mundane a high-quality finish has been applied: the man cleaning the window, nearest the camera, is clearly reflected in the paintwork.

Right: Almost twelve months later, at an exhibition at Euston designed to promote camping coach holidays, one of these vehicles was displayed and here we see members of the LMS staff simulating a mealtime, for interested onlookers. Although converted from its initial purpose, the coach interior retains many interesting original features, such as the ornate carvings and mouldings in the clerestory ceiling, and on the end wall just visible at the end of the corridor.

Right: As the prospect of war loomed larger in the late 1930s the fear of gas attacks, plus the need to be prepared to cope with air raids, led to co-operation between the Home Office and the LMS. Two coaches, painted bright yellow, were designated as an air raid train and here we see an instruction class in process in the decontamination coach of the train at Euston Station on November 24 1937. The poster on the end wall gives advice on the treatment of mustard gas burns.

Left, above: During the early months of World War II there was a constant fear of spies and the consequent need to avoid careless talk. As part of a nationwide campaign, warning posters were placed in passenger-carrying compartments of LMS trains and in this December 9 1939 view we see a porter posting up a notice which reads: "WARNING: Thousands of lives were lost in the last war because valuable information was given away to the enemy through careless talk. BE ON YOUR GUARD." The same warning notice has also been pasted over the decorative print above the seats. The small rectangular notice above the top left-hand corner of the print reads, 'Zebrand, West Africa', while the communication cord notice above the window warns of a £6 penalty for improper use.

Left, below: The provision of railway ambulance trains was an important part of the preparation for the impending conflict. Photographed in October 1939 this interior view shows an unidentified full brake carriage fitted-out and forming part of an hospital train.

Left: A specially posed picture of an ambulance team and their coach, which is former LNWR third class brake No.6321 (pre-1933 LMS No.6504). These vehicles carried various LNWR numbers in the series 6504–7857, and 83 examples were built in 1913: they were 57ft in length and weighed 28 tons. They were originally fitted-out with a brake-end, five compartments (providing 40 seats) and a lavatory.

Right: Shortly before the outbreak of the war in 1939, there was a concerted effort to evacuate school children from the major cities which were judged to be prime air raid targets. In late August 1939 London school children are leaving Blackhorse Road, between South Tottenham and Walthamstow. They are travelling in a Midland Railway non-corridor composite carriage, LMS No.17397, formerly MR No.3363. One of four vehicles built in 1909 to Lot 711, the carriage was designed for the St Pancras-Beford service. The type survived the war, and the last examples were withdrawn in 1955.

Left: The final picture in this section shows members of the British Expeditionary Force returning home from Dunkirk on May 31 1940. The train has stopped somewhere near London and these clearly happy men are being greeted with fruit and cigarettes. They are travelling in a LNWR arc-roof corridor third class carriage built between 1898 and 1903 to D 268, a 50ft vehicle which was originally gas lit. Whilst it is not possible to be sure of its original LNWR number, its first LMS number was 5034 whilst after 1933 it became No.2436.

THE LMS employed around 38,000 men in the locomotive department and if we take the March 1935 figures, these break down into 12,672 drivers, 12,063 firemen, 3,365 cleaners and 5,561 shed staff and other grades. In some respects 1935 was not a wholly average year, because the numbers are much lower than for both 1929 and 1938. The figures for these years are almost identical in so far as footplate staff are concerned and in March 1938 the LMS employed 14,560 drivers, 13,818 firemen, 3,071 cleaners and 5,802 shed staff and other grades. The notable difference between 1938 when compared with 1928, is that the shed staff and other grades are reduced in numbers, due no doubt to the economies achieved during the 1930s as a result of the motive power modernisation and reorganisation programme which was designed to cut costs. This took effect from 1933. An ideal starting point for this section is the men who worked the locomotives which hauled the trains.

'PICTURE POST' magazine, which disappeared from the news stands on June 1 1957, will be fondly remembered by many readers. Published weekly, the magazine specialised in high-quality photo-journalism and a 'Picture Post' story took the reader 'behind the scenes' of a wide variety of subjects and occupations. The magazine depicted Britain's railways from many different points of view over the years, and in 1949 a 'PP' photographer spent some time with a set of Willesden men, and the resulting photographs provide a fascinating glimpse of footplate conditions in the steam years.

Right, above: At 5.30am Driver Bill Perry (right) and Fireman Bill Deal are ready to start their day's work as enginemen. Although taken in the second year of the BR regime, the pictures are purely LMS in essence, and this picture illustrates the footplate 'uniform'. The LMS, unlike the GWR, provided trousers with a bib front for its crews and LMS men, by and large, wore their jackets in the conventional manner, whereas the GWR tradition was to wear braces over the overall top. The LMS shiny-top cap also made good sense: oil and grease could be wiped off easily and did not permanently soil the cap. As might be expected, the fireman's boots are badly scuffed, but the driver has been busy with polish and brushes. The fireman is carrying his tea-can in his left hand, and the bundle under his arm is almost certainly his handbrush, wrapped in a rag.

Right, below: Another highly evocative scene, as Perry and Deal pick their way across the tracks, en-route to their day's work. Footplate work involved many aspects of duty and in some instances a crew would 'book on', prepare their locomotive, carry out their work and then return to the shed. At other times a preparation crew would get the engine ready

FOOTPLATEMEN AND ENGINE SHEDS

for traffic and with all the hard work done, another crew would take over and set off immediately to collect their train. A third alternative was to 'book on', and travel, usually on foot but sometimes 'on the cushions' as passengers to find their train and relieve the crew whose period of duty was at an end. Frequently the original crew were on overtime by the time the relief crew arrived. Perry and Deal are apparently walking to the station to relieve a crew, and they will probably soon be back on shed with a locomotive to 'put away' or 'dispose', both expressions being used to describe the tedious and dirty task of cleaning the fire, raking out the ashpan, emptying the smokebox, filling the tanks with water and the bunker with coal. Crews making their way amongst the tracks like this had be wary and alert — note the signal wires immediately to the left of Perry's feet — ever ready to trip the unwary. At night the dangers were even more intense.

Right: Driver Perry examines the locomotive arrangement board in the dingy lobby of his home shed. This board listed all locomotive turns and the Running Shed Foreman would chalk in the numbers of engines allocated to each duty. At large sheds the board would also carry details of where engines were stabled. Note the footstool to enable the RSF to reach the top of the board with his chalk! The rack on the end wall carried crew timecards with which they 'clocked on and off' using the clock immediately in front of Driver Perry.

Below: Driver Perry and Fireman Deal have located their engine and are getting to grips with the first 'brew' of the day. Deal's tea-can is much larger than the billy-can favoured by most enginemen — this pair obviously had a substantial thirst! Tea was an essential element of daily sustenance aboard a steam locomotive, and in this picture the cup carries the letters LMS. This picture was taken aboard a Horwich 'Crab' 2–6–0.

Below, right: This was without doubt a picture posed by the photographer. The fireman, who looks distinctly uncomfortable, would normally be sitting on his seat and his shovel ought to be in the tender. Furthermore, it is doubtful that he would be hanging on to the injector steam valve handle, other than to avoid toppling over whilst the picture was taken! The crew's seats on a 'Crab' bore a marked resemblance to a modern bar stool and were curious in that they sprouted from the cab floor on a single central leg.

Left: A very typical fireman's view of his mate, who is talking to the 'bobby', as signalmen were frequently known. The signalbox, of LNWR origin (possibly Euston No.2 box), is badly in need of a repaint. This picture was taken aboard a Stanier locomotive: note the spring-loaded doors between engine and tender, which were a marked improvement to the cab doors fitted by Fowler to his locomotives.

Above, left: Bill Perry was driving Stanier '5' 4–6–0 hauling a goods train on the day in 1949 when this series of pictures were taken, and here he is apparently awaiting a clear road ahead after being 'put inside' a loop to allow a more important train to pass. Perry is looking at his pocket watch, and while this picture was also probably staged for the photographer's benefit, goods train crews frequently had to pass time in loops for long periods in circumstances like these. The fire would be put in order and the boiler filled, enabling the crew to take the air and relax on a neighbouring embankment. In this picture a train is signalled to pass on the fast line.

Above, right: Perry and Deal make their way along a narrow 'back alley' of the sort which once provided access to engine sheds all over the country. Sheds were often approached through a maze of back streets and alleyways and this picture will strike a chord for many people. Deal's knapsack was a common enough sight amongst footplatemen, but wicker baskets were less frequently seen.

Right: Perry and Deal are now off-duty and entering the barracks where they will lodge overnight. Before World War II lodging turns were commonplace and frequently disliked by many engine crews. In those days official barracks were frequently located in less-than-desirable locations — adjacent to noisy shunting yards for example — whilst at other locations where men lodged there was no alternative but to take private lodgings. These varied in quality and it was not unknown for both men to have to sleep in the same bed. This was one aspect of the harsh reality which lay behind the romantic notions which some enthusiasts have for the steam era. It was a hard life which would not be accepted today.

Below: It is probable that comparatively few footplatemen were able to 'wash up' in neat and clean surroundings like those shown in this picture. Usually crews had to make the best of a bucket into which hot water was supplied via the engine's 'slacking' pipe. Most footplatemen carried a small towel and a bar of soap in their 'kitbag', but mirrors over a washbasin? — normally unheard of!

Above, right: Enginemen frequently took their meals on the footplate, and facilities of this nature and quality were probably the exception rather than the rule. Many mess rooms were dark, dingy places usually dominated by the fire, or stove, upon which a large kettle full of near-boiling water, for brewing tea, was the most important and permanent feature.

Right: Driver Perry plays close attention whilst a shed fitter grits his teeth as he makes adjustments with a hefty spanner. He is apparently attending to one of the mountings to which part of the reversing gear is attached — although it must be remembered that this scene also could have been staged by the railwaymen for the photographer's benefit.

Below: Driver Perry 'books off' and fills in the 'repair card' with details of any faults he might have noticed on his engine during his duty. This was a serious business on which the fitters attentions were based. However, on occasions a repair card might be found to read: "Whistle needs jacking up and new engine placed beneath it." Some enginemen retained a sense of humour even after a particularly difficult duty!

Above: Very much a posed picture with a self-conscious Driver Perry, who has his hand on the steam regulator. Normally he would be looking forward, with his right hand on the regulator, or if he was using his left hand on the handle, then almost certainly the locomotive would be in reverse gear. The fire doors are open and a very low fire is in evidence. The smoke deflector plate, which is fitted to the top half of the firehole, can just be seen together with the 'bottom plate' which is hanging down. This could be lifted up to cover about half the firehole: this restricted the amount of cold air drawn into the firebox whilst the engine was working, but allowed the fireman to add more coal to the grate. From the arrangements of the controls it is possible to see that this locomotive is a 'Crab' 2–6–0 and the other controls are; drivers brake valve (just in front of his nose) and the live steam valve for the live steam injector (just to the right of the brake valve). Between the live steam valve and the regulator handle can be seen the water gauge with its shut-off and drain cocks. The second water gauge, with the water gauge lamp alongside, is to the right of the regulator handle. The handle between the regulator and right-hand water gauge is the steam blower, used to create draught on the fire.

Left, below: The working day is over and it is time for a chat and a pint of two of beer, perhaps a game of snooker. Time to compare 'Scots' and 'Jubilees', share a joke and exchange yarns. It was a tough job on the footplate, but enginemen forged strong bonds of friendship and camaraderie.

Right: This was a far more typical 'mess' than that illustrated on page 88. This example is small, grubby and dominated by the cast-iron stove and its pair of blackened kettles. You can almost smell the coal-dust and oil!

These two pictures of a gang of young cleaners at work on a 'Patriot' 4–6–0 yield some interesting detail. The front view shows the chain which prevented the smokebox door opening too wide. One man appears to be cleaning the boiler tubes (using a brush mounted on a long rod) while the others are engaged upon general cleaning. It is obviously a hot day, as the lads have all taken off their shirts. The view from the rear is most interesting: first of all note the spick and span tidiness of the track, pits and paved areas. On a long run it was important to get as much coal as possible onto these 3,500-gallon Fowler tenders and two cleaners are busily trimming the coal. The lad standing up has a coal pick, a most useful tool for the fireman — especially when the coal comes in such huge 'cobs' as shown here. The fire-irons are stowed untidily on the rear of the tender, for when fully coaled it was not possible to carry them on their normal brackets, which are partially buried in this view. (See also page 43). In these circumstances the irons had to be stowed on the back filler platform — well out of the fireman's reach, should he actually need them 'on the road'. The lugs used for lifting shackles during works visits are visible on the rear bulkhead.

Left: The view from the driving seat of an unidentified Stanier 'Pacific' as it waits to leave Euston with a northbound express. The field of vision is extremely restricted, which emphasises the degree of concentration and detailed route-knowledge required by top link drivers. The row of holes in the firebox cladding plates, above the handrail, gave access to washout plugs which could be removed to allow powerful water hoses to be inserted during routine boiler washing. The large diameter steel pipe beneath the handrail carried exhaust steam from the ejector (visible immediately in front of the window) which created the vacuum required to operate the continuous train brake.

Above: An interesting comparative view, as seen by the drivers of diesel-electric LMS 'twins' Nos.10000 and 10001. Just under the bridge is a Stanier 'Pacific', probably backing-down from Camden shed to work an express.

Left: On November 6 1935 'Jubilee' class 5XP 4–6–0 No.5552 *Silver Jubilee* was rostered to work a special train to convey HRH the Duke of Gloucester and Lady Alice Montagu-Douglas-Scott on their honeymoon journey from London to Kettering, and the engine is seen here being cleaned for this prestigious job. No.5552 is carrying the Royal train four-lamp headcode, and this is a little puzzling as this headcode was reserved for the sovereign. The mechanical lubricator, driven from the reciprocating motion by a ratchet arrangement, is clearly visible on the running boards. The small-bore pipes emerging from the lubricator carried oil to the cylinders and axleboxes. One further point worthy of notice is that from this angle the front-to-rear 'seam' in the boiler lagging plates is clearly visible.

Left: Another specially posed but nevertheless very appealing photograph, taken on August 16 1943, shows a group of women volunteers cleaning locomotives during their spare time at the weekend. The original caption suggested that hundreds of volunteers all over the country were similarly engaged, which was probably stretching the truth! From the right, the engines are: Class 5 4–6–0 No.5280, class 4F 0–6–0 No.3990, and class 5XP 'Jubilee' No.5682 *Trafalgar*, a mixture which suggests a London, Midland Division depot, probably Kentish Town.

Below: Probably taken on the same day as the picture above, a group of volunteer men are hard at work on Stanier 2–6–2T No.92. Without doubt cleaning locomotives was a very messy business.

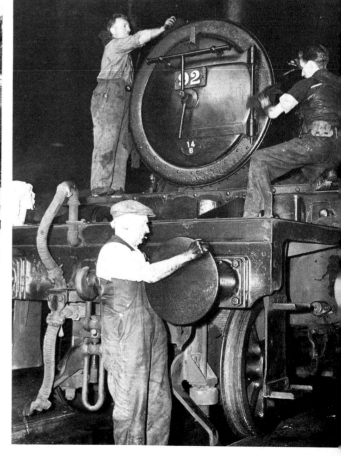

Above: This fascinating photograph was taken at Bletchley on October 2 1935 to illustrate that it was the only engine shed in the country to shoe railway horses. Blacksmith William Thomas, had been a 'smithy' since the age of 13 and a railway employee since 1905. At this time Bletchley possessed a considerable number of subsheds, namely Oxford, Cambridge, Aylesbury, Leighton Buzzard, and Newport Pagnell. The newly-built Stanier class 8 2–8–0 is in fact still a class 7F, as indicated by the power classification painted below the cab windows. The first batch, built with domeless boilers, were classified as '7F' and it was a little later before they became class 8F. Furthermore, apart from the first batch, all class 8F 2-8-0s were built with domed boilers with a separate top feed and not with the top feed, as on No.8008. The 2–8–0 is carrying a 'Not to be moved' sign, from the driver's window, to protect the fitters.

MODERNISATION AT CRICKLEWOOD

THE LMS had been in existence for several years before it could tackle the problem of its less-than-efficient motive power depots, and it wasn't until the 1930s that this problem was taken in hand. In 1926 an Engine History Card procedure had been introduced, whereby the repair costs of every locomotive could be recorded, and this had prompted the early demise of locomotives which were expensive to maintain. In addition to looking at individual engine costs, it was felt that if the time spent on servicing could be reduced, then the time each locomotive spent in revenue-earning service would increase and that this would lead to a reduction in the total number of locomotives required — with attendant savings.

A study of the time spent on shed duties indicated that this was an area where very considerable savings could be made and the principal aims behind the improvement scheme were: greater operating efficiency,

with increased reliability and availability of locomotives; elimination of lost motion, wasteful energy and delay; increasing the number of locations where work could be brought to the men and not vice-versa; reduction of physical effort by the work force. These studies led to the following suggestions for areas where improvements could be made: the provision of coal and water (simultaneously if possible); ash pit work; turning; the stabling of locomotives, either 'on shed' or on preparation pits for their next duty; obtaining greater technical efficiency to reduce casualties in service; the provision of modern machinery for running repairs at sheds; the equipping of as many turntables as possible for mechanical operation; the introduction of a completely new organisation and maintenance structure for the entire motive power department, specifically designed to meet the new criteria.

Cricklewood, originally known as

Childs Hill (the name was changed circa 1900) was one of the first engine sheds to be modernised under the new scheme, and not surprisingly, the press went along to photograph this new development. Six pictures all taken on August 26 1932 illustrate changes which had taken place and the newly installed equipment in operation. The shed itself was located next to the main Edgware Road (known as the A5) and to the east lay the Brent loaded-and-empty wagon sidings, which themselves were separated from each other by the main running lines from St Pancras to St Albans. Principally a 'freight shed', Cricklewood became the destination for the Beyer-Garratt 2–6–0+0–6–2s employed upon the Toton/Wellingborough-London coal trains and it may well have been for this reason that the depot was one of the first to be improved as the 'pilot' for this new scheme. The arrival of the 'Garratts' brought the Company's shed problem into sharp focus, for a few of these massive machines would cause much congestion during servicing.

Grubby LMS Beyer-Garratt 2–6–0+0–6–2 No.4969 is coaled at Cricklewood, by the new coaling plant, on August 26 1932. Lessons learned during the modernisation at this shed in 1932 were incorporated into the MPD improvement programme implemented by the LMS in 1933. No.4969, built as Beyer Peacock No.6650 in 1930, is fitted with a rotary bunker designed to make life easier 'on the road'

for firemen. These were not trouble-free however and could become jammed. This locomotive, as BR No.47969, was withdrawn from Hasland shed in August 1957, and scrapped the same month at Crewe works. Much interesting detail for the modeller in this scene includes the 'catwalk' alongside the delivery chutes, the gas lamp and the tubs of coal being hoisted up the side of the plant to top up its bunker.

Right: Fowler class 7F 0–8–0 No.9627 approaches the coaling tower at Cricklewood on August 26 1932. Not only does this picture give a good idea of the size of this tower, but it also shows an 'Austin Seven', as these large freight locomotives were known. When first constructed (1929–1932) many were to be found on the Midland Division but in their final years they were almost entirely confined to the Central Division, which mostly comprised lines which previously belonged to the old Lancashire & Yorkshire Railway. As BR No.49627 this locomotive was withdrawn from Agecroft Shed in October 1961: it was cut up for scrap at Horwich works the same month. The class (original LMS Nos.9500–9674) was made extinct in December 1961 with the withdrawal of No.49508 (LMS No.9508; from Agecroft. The last survivor was scrapped at Crewe works in February 1962: there are no survivors in preservation.

Left: It was important to keep the dust to a minimum during servicing, and this sprinkler system was installed to ensure that the coal was thoroughly wet before it was tipped into the mechanical coaling plant. Automated coaling saved a great deal of time and labour, compared with previous systems, whereby tubs were filled manually and tipped into tenders, but one disadvantage was that rough mechanical handling often turned good quality coal like this into dust and 'slack'. This was a major reason why the GWR, which used soft Welsh steam coal, never used mechanical coaling methods. A final point of interest in this picture is that at least two 'Garratts' are visible in the centre distance, beyond the sprinkler.

Left: Unlike later designs of mechanical coaling plant, which lifted wagons bodily to the top of the structure, before tipping their contents directly into the storage hoppers, the Cricklewood coaler tipped wagonloads of coal into an underground bunker, from where it was fed into small skips, which were hoisted up the side of the plant, and tipped into the storage hoppers. In this view, from the top of the plant, a wagon is being tipped into the underground hopper, as a loaded skip is winched up the guide rails. As might be expected for a publicity picture, the coal is of very good quality and the five-plank wagon is in exceptionally good condition.

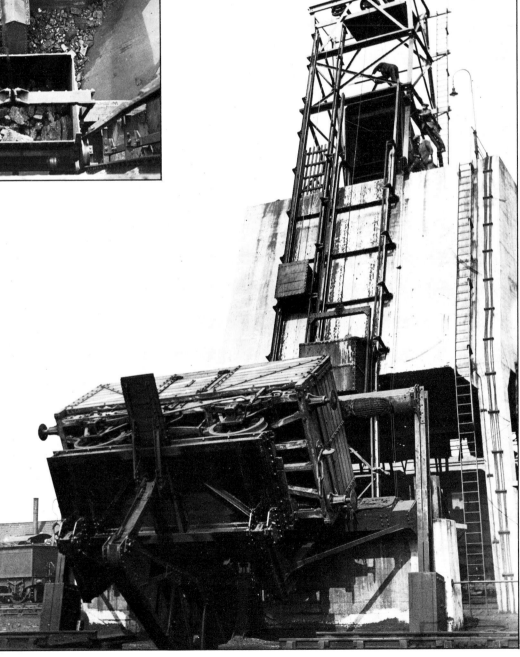

Right: A more conventional view of the scene depicted above, and a picture which reveals much detail about the construction of both the concrete plant itself and the wagon tippler. The skip containing coal bound for the storage hopper is visible, although partially obscured by the corner of the wagon: the counterweights used to ease the load on the electric winch are just descending, slightly above and to the left. The plant was equipped with two storage hoppers, of 100 tons and 50 tons capacity, enabling differing grades of fuel to be stored, and each hopper supplied twin 'jigger' feeds, enabling four locomotives (or two 'Garratts') to be coaled simultaneously. Accidents do happen and it was not unknown for wagon loads of commodities other than coal to be tipped into mechanical plants. At Steamtown, Carnforth, where a later design of mechanical plant survives in working order, former railwaymen recall with wry humour an occasion when a wagon load of full oil drums was tipped into the hopper.

Right: Shoeburyness, on the LT&S section of the Midland Division, was the terminal point of the intensive commuter services from Fenchurch Street. In addition to this regular traffic, Southend also attracted excursions not only from London, but from all over the LMS system and the very busy depot was therefore an early candidate for modernisation. This picture, taken in August 1933, shows the newly-built coaling plant, just before it was commissioned. In certain respects the tower differed from the type normally intended for secondary depots. With a capacity of 100 tons, it had three 'jigger' feeds, a design feature which probably reflected the depot's motive power allocation, which in 1945 was: 22 2–6–4Ts, two 0–6–2Ts and seven 4–4–2T locomotives — there was not a tender engine to be found.

Below: LNWR 'Claughton' 4–6–0 No.1334 is mechanically coaled at Camden in 1926. Built in 1917, this locomotive became LMS No.5936 and ran only until 1932, when it was withdrawn. Many of the 'Claughton' 4–6–0s had very short lives, as the joint result of the reduction of traffic in the early 1930s, and the arrival of the new and more economical Stanier locomotives. The engine is coupled to LNWR tender No.1841, and the small oval plate bearing the number 15, attached to the rear edge of the cab roof, indicated that the engine was allocated to Crewe.

Right: Photographed on January 29 1924, the original caption to this highly evocative picture reads: "This morning drivers and firemen who have been on strike were busy preparing their engines ready to get back to work." Probably not specially posed (not a soul to be seen!) the picture provides an excellent typical view of a busy engine shed, namely the west end of Camden, the LNWR's London passenger locomotive depot. Unfortunately, the individual locomotives cannot be identified; however, the 4–4–0 on the left appears to be a saturated 'Precursor', while the other two engines are almost certainly superheated 'George the Fifth' 4–4–0s. The locomotive on the right is 'blowing off' and ready for service.

Left: During the General Strike of May 1926, some railway services were worked by volunteers and here we see a group of volunteers at Camden, preparing three 'Claughton' 4-6-0s for duty. It is not possible to identify the two engines on the right, but the locomotive on the left appears to be No.6001, an un-named example, built in 1920, which previously carried LNWR No.23. The 4–6–0 is painted in crimson lake livery, with LMS lettering on the cabside, this style being used in 1923 on a number of LNWR locomotives until the LMS emblem became available. No.6001 later ran with an ROD type tender, before being withdrawn in 1934, after just 14 years service — a very short life for an engine of that era.

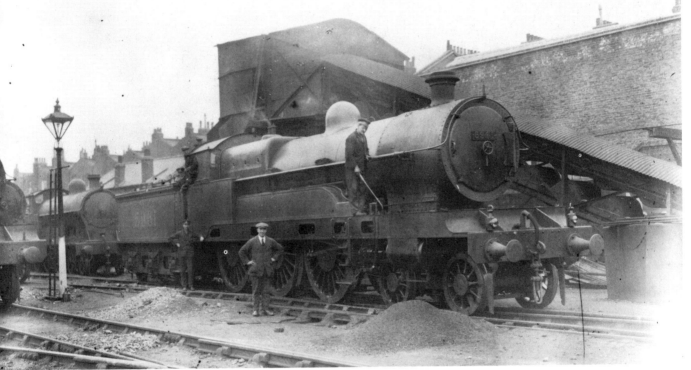

Above: 'Claughton' 4–6–0 No.5961 is prepared for duty by volunteers at Camden on May 14 1926 during the General Strike. The man on the running boards is holding a long oiler, which allowed him to lubricate parts of the inside motion without climbing between the main frames. No.5961 was built in 1920 as LNWR No.178, and was withdrawn in 1934.

Left: Looking very dour, Driver A. Pink fills the oil cups on the upper slidebar of an unidentified 4–6–0 on August 31 1927. Note the vacuum exhauster, mounted beneath the lower slidebar, and connected to the crosshead by a single arm. Stanier eventually abandoned these exhausters in favour of a small ejector, for the maintenance of vacuum for train brakes. The pipes emerging from the bottom of the cylinder were linked to the drain cocks, (or 'taps' as they were better known), used to keep the cylinders free of condensed water.

Right: A group of schoolboys studying communications visit Willesden shed roundhouse in 1947. Willesden had always been largely a freight engine depot and while the presence of a large passenger tank locomotive is therefore a little unrepresentative, a number of the type were allocated to the shed, and two-cylinder Stanier Class 4P 2–6–4T No.2590 may have been one. This class was introduced in 1935 and a total of 206 locomotives were built; No.2590 was constructed by the North British Locomotive Company, in 1936. One feature of this class was that the water pickup scoop could operate in both directions

Below: The visit of a group of Swedish Railway employees, who spent five months on a study tour of British railways, was the reason the Topical Press photographer recorded this scene at Camden Town Motive Power Depot, on February 8 1934. Class 4P 4–4–0 'Compound' No.1106 was one of the standard 'Compounds' based on the original MR design — but with added superheating — which became an early LMS standard class. Splendid locomotives, they were a little too small for the heaviest duties but nevertheless performed well, once their 'non-Midland' crews had become accustomed to them. Camden's allocation was considerable and they were frequently used on the two-hour London-Birmingham expresses, until displaced by the later Stanier 4–6–0s. A total of 195 examples were built for the LMS, No.1106 being built in 1925 at Derby and withdrawn in 1958.

Below: There was very little glamour attached to railway work. The hours were long, the conditions could be awful when compared with the modern day environment and the pay was not over-generous. Nevertheless, it was not until the post-1945 period that labour became scarce as a result of better-paid jobs, with better conditions, existing elsewhere. Shed fitters and boilersmiths worked in particularly unpleasant conditions and in this picture a member of the shed staff is inside a locomotive firebox examining the tubes above the brick arch. The large diameter flue tubes carried the superheater elements. The purpose of the brick arch was to protect the tubeplate and tube-ends from the direct flame of the fire. During intervals of firing when the firebox temperature falls, the brick arch radiates heat which helps prevent leaks developing as a result of rapid fluctuations in the tubeplate temperature. The brick arch also promotes thorough combustion of the gaseous products of the fuel, by lengthening their path from the fire-grate to the tube plate. At the same time, and acting in conjunction with the firehole deflector plate, it also causes these burning gases to be thoroughly mixed with the supply of secondary or 'top air', admitted to the firebox through the firehole door. Boilersmiths frequently had to enter a firebox to carry out minor repairs when the fire had only recently been removed — and it was not unknown for repairs to be carried out with the fire pushed under the arch when an engine was urgently required back in service. Note how heat from the fire has melted the lower surface of the arch to form miniature 'stalactites'.

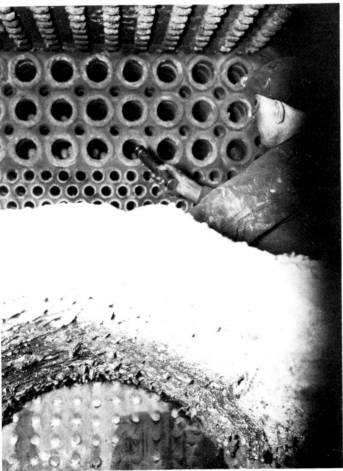

Top: Drivers had a lengthy preparation procedure to carry out before their locomotives could leave the shed, and this involved detailed inspection and lubrication of all moving parts. Carried out every day, the drivers' inspection ensured that all wheels, axleboxes, valve gear and brake rigging were in good condition and that the engine was safe to run. Smokebox and firebox tubeplates were similarly examined, for leaks. Drivers usually carried out their inspection as they 'oiled round' an engine and in this view on April 30 1932, an engineman has climbed up between the main frames of a 'Royal Scot' 4–6–0 to lubricate the inside big end and other moving parts associated with the middle cylinder. This could be a highly dangerous practice.

Above: Also taken on April 30 1932, this carefully posed shot also purports to show a driver preparing a 'Royal Scot' 4–6–0 for a record-breaking run to Scotland. This is an unusual view of the 'Scot' motion, with the big end and connecting rod immediately in front of the lens. Everything is immaculately clean: not a speck of dirt or drop of oil to be seen anywhere on the rods, wheels or framing.

RAILCARS
AND
DIESEL & ELECTRIC TRACTION

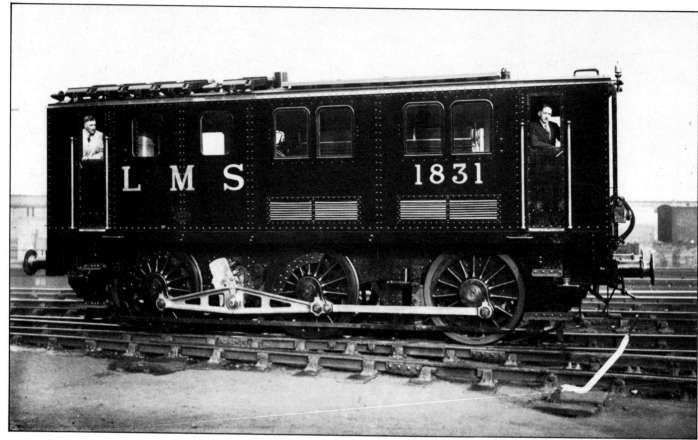

IT WAS not difficult to see why steam shunting locomotives were an early target for the economy seekers. A steam shunting locomotive could operate for about 24 hours, but during this time it required three different two-man crews — three drivers and three firemen.

If we examine a typical day we find that set No. 1 books on at 6.00am to prepare the locomotive, being ready to depart from the shed by 6.45am. Thus nearly one hour of the shift has passed before the business of shunting can begin. Depending upon a variety of circumstances, their relief will 'book on' sometime between 1.00pm and 2.00pm but prior to the changeover of crews the 'morning shift' will have ceased shunting in order to clean the fire and prepare the locomotive for the changeover. A third set of relief men, who form the night shift, will book on between 9.00–10.00pm and the pre-changeover fire cleaning will have taken place once again. The night men bring the locomotive back

to the shed and depending upon the circumstances either they or a set of 'disposal men' will 'put it away' — clean the fire, rake out the ashpan, empty the smokebox fill the tank and coal the locomotive.

The advantages which a diesel locomotive or shunter offered were:- single-manning (except when running on the main lines), continuous operation (no fire cleaning), able to stay out working for a week, and unlike a steam locomotive which burned coal and used water, even when not working, a diesel could be shut down when not required. With all these potential advantages to be achieved, it was not surprising that in the 1930s the LMS turned attention to alternatives to steam shunting locomotives and the locomotive illustrated above represents the first experiment in this direction.

At Derby Works in February 1932 the engineers took MR 0–6–0T No. 1831 and 'converted' it into a diesel hydraulic locomotive. The engine unit

Above: 0–6–0 diesel-hydraulic shunting locomotive No.1831, built at Derby in 1932 (Works No.8071). The locomotive was constructed using parts of 0–6–0T No.1831 and the steam parentage is clear. Note also the cooling radiators on the left-hand end of the cab roof, and the small whistle at the opposite end, operated by the locomotive's air system. No.1831 survived until September 1939, after which it was scrapped.

was a six-cylinder heavy fuel oil four-stroke unit of 400bhp, running at 750rpm and was supplied by Davey-Paxman of Colchester, while Messrs. Haslom & Newton of Derby supplied the transmission. Two driving compartments were provided, one at each end of the unit, with duplicated controls on each side of the cab. No. 1831 was not entirely satisfactory in service however, considerable problems being encountered with the gearbox. It was eventually withdrawn in 1939 and converted into a Mobile Power Unit.

Right: This publicity view taken at Crewe in 1936 illustrates a variety of different diesel shunting locomotives built for the LMS. 0–6–0 No.7072 was built in 1936 by Hawthorne Leslie and represents the most modern of the different types of shunters then in service on the LMS. The third locomotive is the Sentinel No.7192.

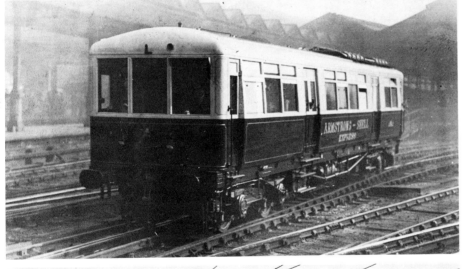

Left: On February 20 1933 the LMS inaugurated Britain's first diesel-electric powered express passenger train — the Armstrong Shell express, which ran between Euston and the British Industries Fair at Castle Bromwich, Birmingham. It is pictured here at Euston. Built by Armstrong-Whitworth and powered by a light 'diesoleum' oil provided by Shell, this experimental single car unit was never taken into LMS stock. The interior layout, on the Pullman style, provided chairs for 12 passengers in two compartments, plus two lavatories, together with a kitchen and pantry. In addition, the passenger compartments were provided with a speedometer by which progress could be monitored. Speeds above 60mph were maintained, with a maximum of 70mph being achieved. During the course of the fair the car recorded a creditable running cost of 0.71 pence per mile.

Left, below: A four-car electric multiple unit train, on the 8½-mile Manchester and Altrincham line on May 11 1931, the first day of operation following its conversion from steam to electric traction. The Manchester South Junction & Altrincham Railway was, until 1947, owned jointly by the LMS and the LNER and when it was electrified in 1931 it became the first passenger line in Britain to utilise the 1500 Volt DC overhead supply system. The new stock was built to LMS style, but using 58ft underframes, the only LMS coaches ever built to this length. Constructed by Metropolitan-Cammell with Metro-Vick equipment, a total of 22 three-car sets were built, comprising motor brake third, composite trailer and driving trailer formation, together with two spare motor brake third class vehicles. The stock was given MSJA numbers and livery: a mid-green body lined in LMS period II style

Left: The French Micheline Tyre Company developed the concept of a flanged rail wheel with a rubber tyre, and trials in France led to an invitation by the LMS to the Micheline company to test one of its petrol-engined vehicles on the LNWR Oxford—Bletchley branch, in February 1932. On February 9 that year we see the railbus stabled at Oxford LNWR shed, under scrutiny by an LMS driver who is also pictured in close-up (below), supposedly examining the tyres. The road vehicle ancestry of this railbus is very clear, and one disadvantage was that the vehicle needed turning to face its destination.

The LMS operating authorities were unconvinced by the vehicle shown above, partly because it was too light to be fitted with the conventional draw gear needed to attach an extra coach, van or wagon if required at busy times. However, in March 1934 this larger, improved railbus was brought from France for testing, with the aim of running between Oxford and Cambridge. Pictured here on February 18 1935, the vehicle was 45ft in length, weighed 9½ tons (extensive use of aluminium in the bodywork kept weight to a minimum) and could seat 56 passengers. The 16-wheeled vehicle was capable of more than 60mph, powered by a Hispano Suiza 240bhp petrol engine. All wheels were fitted with pressure gauges, and any loss of pressure caused a hooter to sound in the cab, and a steel rim inside the tyre prevented the tyre collapsing in the event of complete deflation. Two spare tyres were carried. The Armstrong Siddeley company, of Coventry, became interested in the Micheline principle and in conjunction with the French company and the LMS, agreed to build two further 56-seat vehicles (see page 104), and consequently 'Coventy Railcar' crests were applied to the French-built vehicle.

Left: A detail view of the French railcar's trailing eight-wheel 'bogie', clearly showing the two spare wheels carried by the vehicle. In the event of a puncture, it was claimed that the defective tyre could be changed within minutes using spanners and jacking equipment carried by the vehicle. The thought of a driver, crouched in the ballast to jack up his train and change a wheel is nevertheless an intriguing one! Note the track-circuit contact 'shoes' between the wheels. The April 1935 issue of 'The Railway Magazine' reported: "On a recent test, the car ran from Leighton Buzzard to Euston, 40.2 miles, in 42½ min., with a maximum speed of 66mph. The running was very steady and silent."

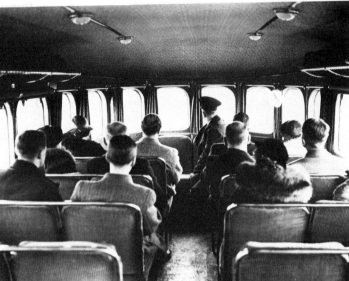

Left: Posed by the Topical photographer, this interesting picture emphasises the raised 'cab' of the Micheline railbus, which overcame the need to turn this vehicle. The roller door gave access to the vehicle's 15-cwt capacity luggage compartment. The French-built railcar's driving cab was only slightly offset from the centreline, whereas the Coventry-built vehicles' cabs were located on the extreme offside, as illustrated overleaf.

Above: An interior view of one of the Coventry-Micheline railbuses, showing upholstery, lighting and decorative detail.

Top: Coventry Railcar No.1 stands at Coventry station on June 22 1936. Neatly blocking the view of the interested spectators on the platform is an unidentified LNWR 2–4–2T, fitted for motor train work, while standing beyond the car is an unidentified Class 4F 0–6–0. The railcar itself featured various items of special interest. Three of the four axles on each bogie were driven through a four-speed gearbox, and there was a shaft drive to each first axle with double roller chains to the second and third axles. The reversing gear was operated by dog clutches in a steel casing. Power was provided by an Armstrong Siddeley 275bhp engine, but this was subsequently replaced with an Hispano Suiza engine of 240bhp, due to teething troubles with the original unit. It is not known if the original Armstrong engine was later refitted. Trials followed on the Oxford—Cambridge and the Market Harborough–Rugby lines with the cars being based at Rugby engine shed. Additional service followed in the Rugby, Leamington, Nuneaton and Coventry areas, but the original two cars were the only examples built and it is recorded that they were broken up in 1945. It is worth noting that while this concept was not carried forward in Great Britain, the Micheline idea has been developed in France and on the Paris Metro underground system vehicles ride on pneumatic tyres.

Above, left & right: In 1934 the LMS introduced three Leyland four-wheel railcars, (Nos.29950–52) which were allocated to Diagram 2132. They weighed 10½ tons empty and could carry 40 third class passengers and were somewhat similar in concept to the British Railways railbuses of the late 1950s. As far as known, the livery was crimson lake and cream, with coach transfers for company ownership marking and vehicle number. Originally, they were employed on branch lines in the Accrington, Blackburn, Lower Darwen, Preston and Hamilton areas before all being withdrawn by 1951. This pair of pictures show one of the railcars on display at Euston on February 21 1934. Each of the three cars was powered by a Leyland six-cylinder diesel engine, driving through Lysholm-Smith hydraulic transmission, giving direct drive at top speed. The cars were 38ft long and on a trial run between Euston and Watford, a fully loaded vehicle covered the 17½ mile trip in 24 min 10 sec, maintaining 50mph for much of the distance.

The final LMS experiment with diesel traction before World War II broke out was with an articulated three-coach unit, numbered 80000–2. This distinctive 'streamlined' design was very much in keeping with the fashions of the late 1930s and while originally painted an aluminium colour above the waistline and bright scarlet below, it was altered, as shown (above), to cream and scarlet with a black band and a silver-coloured roof, when it went into revenue-earning traffic. It was 182ft long overall, and seated 54 third class passengers in two saloons in the outer cars, while the centre car, a composite, carried 30 third class passengers in one saloon (below, left) and a further 24 first class passengers in a second, independent saloon. Most seating was fitted transversely, with reversible seat backs. Lavatories and luggage accommodation were provided in each coach. Passenger access was by air-operated centre sliding doors only. The driving cab was spacious and the driver sat centrally, as illustrated (below, right). Following initial trials from Euston, the unit went to work on the Oxford—Cambridge line making three return trips daily stopping at Sandy, Bedford and Bletchley only. The run took but 80 minutes for the 77 miles — which compared well with the steam service of around 180 minutes! During the War the unit was stored at Bedford where it remained until 1949 when the two outer cars, Nos.80000/2 were converted for use as a self-propelled departmental unit for electric overhead installation and maintenance repair work. It was renumbered M198895/6 in the departmental stock series. Note that the unit is not fitted with conventional drawgear, which would have spoiled its streamlined appearance. Also of interest is the brass whistle.

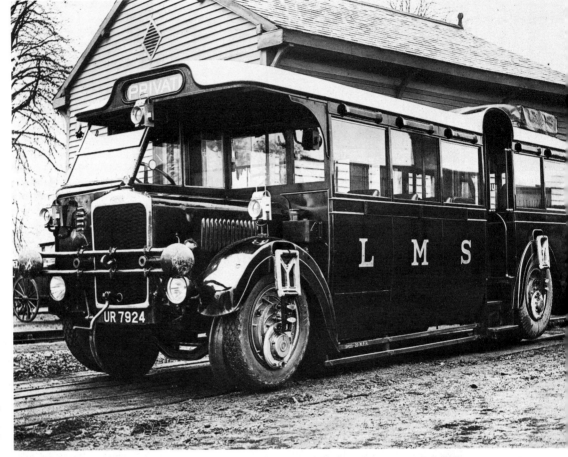

BEFORE leaving the realms of experimental ideas — which were usually rather short lived — we take a brief look at the Karrier 'Ro-Railer', which had a very short life. With bodywork built at Craven's works in Sheffield, in 1931, it entered service on April 1 1932, only to be withdrawn a few weeks later, on July 2. It was initially tested at Redbourn, on the Harpenden—Hemel Hempstead branch, but is more normally associated with its brief period of service on the SMJ section in the Stratford-upon-Avon area.

Top: Specially prepared areas were provided for the Ro-Railer, where the rails were flush with the surface, to enable the vehicle to switch from rail to road traction, and vice-versa.

After arriving at the siding by road, the Ro-Railer was driven over the rails, and then moved forward to the point where the hard-standing tapered away, the rail wheels thus coming into contact with the track and taking the weight of the vehicle. The road wheels, which were mounted on eccentrics, were then cranked half-a-turn to raise them clear for rail use. Note the detachable buffing and drawgear mounted across the radiator, and the supplementary railway lamp fittings. The Ro-

Railer is pictured here on its rail wheels during trials at Redbourn in 1931.

Above, left: The railbus is pictured straddling the rails on its road wheels, ready to be driven forward off the ramped hard-standing, to lower the rail wheels onto the track. The railway lamps are in position, but the 'buffer beam' has been removed from the two mountings, either side of the radiator.

Above, right: With the rail wheels now sitting on the track and the vehicle clear of the hard-standing, a pair of railwaymen demonstrate how the road wheels were cranked clear

of the track, during rail operations. Under operating conditions the change-over could be made in about five minutes: under test conditions this was accomplished in 2½ minutes. The Ro-Railer was fitted with a 120hp (maximum) six-cylinder petrol engine, and a supplementary gearbox gave increased speed at low engine speed on long railway trips. However, the Karrier Road-Railer was really too heavy in relation to its seating capacity and power, though it was mechanically successful in other respects and the wheel changing equipment worked well. When first demonstrated the vehicle, hailed as the 'missing link' in transport, attracted attention from all over the globe.

Above: This final 1931 view at Redbourn depicts trials in progress, watched by officials who had probably travelled from London in an officers special, hauled by '483' class 4–4–0 No.556. For passenger traffic, the Ro-Railer was said to have the following advantages: low running costs, comfort and improved visibility as compared with conventional branch line trains, and journeys shortened and the payment of heavy tolls avoided by railing the vehicle at convenient points. If adapted for goods use, the vehicle would allow a true 'door to door' service, and it was also claimed that railway maintenance gangs could also use Ro-Railer to transport them to their work. The potential was exaggerated however, and the Ro-Railer became little more than an interesting curiosity.

Left: An attractive scene on April 25 1932 at the LMS-owned Welcombe Hotel, Stratford-upon-Avon, as the Karrier Ro-Railer collects passengers and luggage for a trip to Blisworth, to connect with a London train. The rail wheels, manufactured by the Lang Wheel Company, are visible inside the pneumatic-tyred road wheels. The Ro-Railer's seats were staggered to give increased passenger comfort, and some of the rear seats tipped to create extra luggage space. Sanding gear was provided to assist adhesion on greasy rails. The vehicle had access doors on both sides, with steps to assist passengers boarding from ground level, and an arched door frame to provide sufficient headroom for passengers joining from a station platform.

STATISTICS:

Chassis wheelbase	17ft 1in	
Road wheel track	6ft 3½in	
Size of tyres	Front 36in × 6in; Rear 42in × 9in	
Top gear ratio (road)	7 to 1	
Top gear ratio (rail)	4.2 to 1	
Maximum speed (road)	60mph	
Maximum speed (rail)	75mph	
Petrol consumption (road)	8mpg	
Petrol consumption (rail)	16mpg	
Load capacity	26 passengers/3 tons net	
Overall length	26ft	
Overall width	7ft 5in	
Overall height (road)	9ft 9¾in	
Overall height (rail)	9ft 6½in	
Floor to roof height	6ft 4¼in	
Unladen weight (complete)	7tons 2cwt 2 qtr	

Right: An attractive works view of LMS 0–6–0 diesel shunter No.7120, one of a batch of six locomotives built at Derby in 1945, Nos.7120–5, which later became BR Nos.12033–38. Designated as BR class 11, this design was the forerunner of the successful class 08/9 locomotives, which are still active. The LMS series of this design reached No.7131 (BR No.120544), after which locomotives carried only BR numbers, Nos.12045–12138 being built between 1948 and 1952. No.7120 was withdrawn and scrapped in January 1969 and the whole class was extinct by 1972. *Courtesy British Rail.*

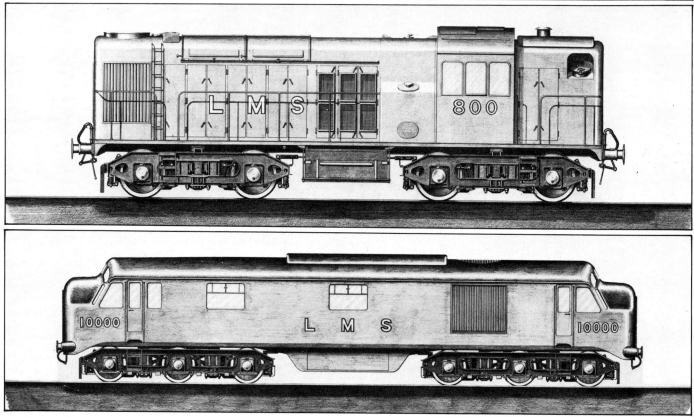

Centre: Issued by the LMS Advertising & Publicity Department on March 21 1947, this artist's impression helped point the way ahead for the Company's aims in the field of diesel traction. This locomotive was described in the original captions as: ". . . a new design 800hp diesel-electric locomotive which the LMS is to introduce experimentally for branch and cross-country passenger and freight services." In the event, this locomotive did not appear until 1950, when it was delivered to British Railways by the North British Locomotive Company of Glasgow, works No.26413. It was a Bo-Bo locomotive of 827hp, carrying the number 10800, and was intended for branch line and secondary services with a maximum speed of 70mph and a maximum tractive effort of 34,500 lb. British Thomson-Houston provided much of the power equipment and the 16-cylinder diesel engine was by Davey Paxman. The locomotive weighed 69 tons 16cwt in running order and was 41ft 10½in in length, over buffers. The locomotive was withdrawn in 1959 and sold to the Brush Traction Company, which renumbered it 710 and whilst the locomotive was known as *Hawk*, it never carried a nameplate. The locomotive was used as a test-bed and was withdrawn following use as a mobile power unit, in 1972. It had been dismantled by February 1976. *Courtesy British Rail.*

Above: Also issued by the Company's Advertising & Publicity Department on March 21 1947, this was the artist's impression of the design which the LMS introduced on the very eve of its extinction, in December 1947, as diesel-electric Co-Co No.10000. Although basically similar in outline to the finished product, this impression was a little wide of the mark in some respects: the nose and cab window design is a little clumsy. *Courtesy British Rail.*

Above: No.10000 leaves St Pancras on a test train, bound for Derby, on January 15 1948. The LMS dynamometer car is coupled next to the locomotive.

Above: On October 5 1948 No.10001, which entered service in July 1948 and thus never carried the LMS lettering applied to its sister engine, pilots No.10000 out of Euston with the 1pm Euston—Glasgow service. This was the first time the 'twins' worked together, and they subsequently became a familiar sight working 'in tandem' on the West Coast main line. The pair were fitted with 16-cylinder English Electric diesel engines, had a tractive effort of 41,400lb and weighed 127½ tons. The locomotives were 61ft 2in in length over buffers and were capable of a top speed of 93mph. Their design paved the way for later more powerful main line diesels and many aspects of their design were developed and re-used. No.10001 was withdrawn in December 1963, No.10000 surviving until March 1966. Unfortunately, neither example was preserved: No.10000 was scrapped by Cashmore's of Great Bridge in 1968, and No.10001 was dismantled by Cox & Danks, Acton, also in 1968.

THE RAILWAY FACTORIES AT:
CREWE & DERBY

WITHOUT doubt the greatest of the Victorian 'railway factories' was Crewe Works, traditionally associated with the London & North Western Railway but in fact created before that Company came into being.

The railway works came to Crewe simply as a result of expansion and it was to the credit of John Moss, chairman of the Grand Junction Railway, that it came about. In 1839 the GJR was growing fast and even at this early date in railway history, personality problems were beginning to appear. In this instance the problem, as seen by the GJR Board, was that Thomas Melling, in charge of the traction side of the business could not cope with the job and therefore Joseph Locke, the Engineer-in-Chief of the GJR, was instructed to reorganise the Locomotive Department and to put it onto a proper footing. At this date the repair shops for locomotives were located in cramped quarters at Edge Hill, Liverpool, some way off the system and built on land rented from the Liverpool & Manchester Railway. Furthermore, the premises were incapable of being reasonably enlarged: the solution was to find a new site and to start again.

At the same time, negotiations were in progress for the GJR to take over the Chester & Crewe Railway, this becoming effective from May 19 1840. One benefit was that the GJR inherited the

C&CR's power to buy land at Crewe and this was a useful asset, because it was at this point that the Manchester & Birmingham Railway was likely to make its junction with the existing railways. The C&CR had already purchased land at Crewe on which it proposed to build workshops, and so it was here that Locke felt the new locomotive works should be located, being fairly central to the system, though without coal or much water handy and certainly far away from any iron workings.

From this point on matters moved quickly; the land was purchased and plans prepared and from 1840 the growth of Crewe began in earnest, and for many years the town and Works were virtually one and the same. In 100 years Crewe's population grew from a mere handful to around 45,000 of whom between 7,000 and 8,000 were employed at the works, with others employed at the steam sheds and marshalling yards. Truly this was a great railway town and, in so far as the works were concerned the new facilities fulfilled the claim of John Moss the GJR chairman who said: "This grand manufactory will be the finest and most extensive railway workshop in the world."

It would be very difficult to find any LMS equipment which, at one time or another, Crewe Works did not make or repair. The list is almost endless. Starting with locomotives, carriages and wagons the works had its own foundry to produce castings and its own steel-plant. It also worked in wood, making signals, and the full list of products would include such diverse items as rails, keys, steel sleepers, chairs, crossings, signal posts (wooden and steel tubular), signal gantries, electric signalling equipment, station and signal lamps, bridge materials, chairs, level crossing gates, carts, huts of all kinds, carts, barrows, office furniture, coal scuttles, soap, marine boilers, grease, pipe-mains for gas, together with town gas, water and sewage systems, iron handles, fences, bricks, artificial limbs of wood and metal, machine tools, cranes, steelworks plant, dynamos, engine shed frames, snowploughs, road transport trailers, turntables, rail tractors, cable drums, and air compressors, whilst in wartime the Works turned its attention to such items as armoured trains

and tanks, together with a wide range of armaments.

In the early years it was necessary to build houses in order to accommodate the workers and their families who were transferred from Liverpool, and a little later the railway-built Christ Church was consecrated. This was the beginning of a great railway Works which became part of the LMS on January 1 1923; however Crewe Works was not a happy place at that particular point in time.

For too long Crewe had followed obsolete practices and in the early post-war years it was evident that the Works standards were not of the highest order. In 1922, in advance of the 1923 Grouping, the LNWR and LYR had amalgamated and this led to George Hughes of the LYR becoming CME of the enlarged system. Inspecting Crewe, he found that the Works' standards of accuracy, measurement and production techniques fell short of those obtained at Horwich on the LYR. During the year that followed Hughes did manage to bring about some improvements at Crewe, which included a more progressive outlook toward modern mechanical engineering, but all too soon it was 1923 and the LMS was born.

The 1920s were troubled years for Crewe works. Beginning with Hughes endeavouring to bring the works up to date, we find that by mid-1923 plans were afoot to reorganise the methods of locomotive repair, as too much time was being wasted, often more than 40 days. In February 1925 the Rolling Stock Committee of the LMS Board agreed the scheme submitted by CME Hughes and work commenced. It had three aims: reorganisation to produce much shorter repair times through a tightly programmed work flow in the erecting shop and the various shops feeding work to the erectors; a reduction in the number of transfer movements within the works area; the rebuilding of the four existing erecting shops and the valve motion shop into a new boiler department that would build all new boilers for all divisions of the LMS.

One 'benefit' of the Grouping was the closure of the old LYR steelmaking plant at Horwich and the concentration of all the LMS steel-making capacity at Crewe by building a new plant, and this was brought into com-

Facing page: This magnificent general view of the Crewe Works erecting shop, in 1934, clearly shows lines — or 'belts' as they were known in the Works — of locomotives under construction and repair. The 'new work belt' on the right comprises new locomotives, whilst on the left are 'belts' of engines under repair. Two LNWR 0–8–0s, an LMS class 3F 0–6–0T, and 0–6–0s of class 4F and LNWR origin are clearly visible in the nearest line of engines under repair, while the engine with LMS lettering on its tank sides in the next row is a 2–4–2T of LYR origin. Note the various components receiving attention on the shop floor: in the foreground are a set of coupling rods and a blastpipe, beyond which can be seen a selection of jacks and stands, a new Stanier cab, boiler cladding sheets, boiler tubes and pipework, and an ashpan. The workshop floor comprises oak blocks set in pitch, which were quickly spirited away as firewood on the occasions they were knocked loose from the floor during repairs!

Right: An everyday scene inside Crewe works on March 12 1931, as heat is applied to the leading part of an 0–6–0's main frames: Fowler '4F' 0–6–0s were prone to sustaining distorted frames behind the buffer beam. Once heated to the correct temperature, the softened frame would be straightened and the steel allowed to cool. The smokebox has been removed and the boiler moved back to allow work to proceed.

Right, below: This 1931 picture illustrates some of the lifting equipment in the Crewe Works erecting shop: the hooks were slipped under buffer beams to lift locomotives quickly and easily during repairs. Note the boy's dress: one-piece boiler suit, cloth cap, no gloves. Behind him is an unidentified LNWR 'Prince of Wales' 4–6–0 under repair.

mission during the mid/late 1920s. However this was not to last long, as the slump of 1929-31 and the need to renew the railmill led to a deal being agreed with the English Steel industry whereby the LMS obtained its steel at a price of 10% less than 'current prices' and this agreement was to last for 10 years. As a result, the LMS closed its own steel mill and more than 400 men lost their jobs. Redundancies on the railways are not a new phenomenon. Shortly afterwards a further economy was the closure of the brickworks. However, wartime conditions led to an increased need for steel and so the Works steelmaking plant was recommissioned in 1941.

The works produced 'town Gas' and in 1925 the gasworks was remodelled and further extensions to those works enabled the production increase needed to supply the townspeople and the Rolls Royce factory which had been established in the town.

However, the principal reorganisation of the 1920s concerned locomotive repairs. LMS Carriage & Wagon Superintendent R. W. Reid visited Crewe Works in 1923 and, like Hughes, saw the urgent need for a thorough overhaul and in February 1925 the Rolling Stock Committee of the LMS Board agreed the scheme submitted by CME Hughes and work commenced. It had three aims: reorganisation to produce much shorter repair times through a tightly programmed work flow in the erecting shop and the various shops feeding work to the erectors; a reduction in the number of transfer movements within the works area; the rebuilding of the four existing erecting shops and the valve motion shop into a new boiler department that would build all new boilers for all divisions of the LMS.

A further improvement was the construction of a new erecting shop which was to handle all new construction and repairs enabling the

Right: Viewed from one of the overhead cranes in the works in 1931, a pair of wheels are mounted in a lathe, and reprofiling of the tyres is in progress. Smoke and swarf is visible around the cutting tools and 'turnings' are accumulating in the bed of the lathe, the sweeping-up of which would doubtless be a job for an apprentice.

Below: Crewe works had a considerable capacity for producing steel: following the construction of the new steel works this amounted to 84,000 tons per year from the two 40/45 ton acid open hearth furnaces and the two 60/70 ton basic open hearth furnaces. In this view we see four tons of molten metal being poured into a mould during casting operations on September 14 1934.

older erecting shops to be converted for other purposes. The new shop had three bays 642ft. long and 63ft. wide and each bay had a central track. All engines for repair were brought in by a 100-ton traverser and were moved first onto the stripping pits, where they remained for two days. When stripping was complete the frame assembly was lifted forward, where it remained for four days for attention by gangs specialising in certain aspects of the work required in these various stages. On the seventh day assembly work began with the re-

placement of the bogies and wheels, with the frames and boiler assembly being lowered onto them. The work on each stage was carefully planned to take 7 hours 50 minutes of working times and the work was moved along by using a steel cable pulled by an electric winch, thus moving the work to the men in a practice which gave rise to the name 'the belt system'. Each 'belt' produced a completely repaired locomotive every working day and an engine was coupled to a repaired tender which had been shunted into position after repair on a

modified belt system used in the tender shop.

One line in the erecting shop was usually occupied with new construction, while a another pit accommodated smaller engines which passed through the works in 10 days instead of the 12 required for the larger machines. With six lines in operation the capacity averaged up to 100 new locomotives per year and 30–35 heavy repairs per week, but within a few years the cable for movement down the line was discontinued except for final haulage into the yard. Internal movement was thereafter made by cranes.

It was during this period of reorganisation that the painting of locomotives ceased at Crewe, which led to the remarkable story that 'Crewe refused to paint its locomotives in the hated Midland red colour'. This story is total nonsense, but it has appeared in print more than once. The facts are that prior to the reorganisation, Crewe had adopted the new livery and as soon as possible it began again, but during this period of works reorganisation about 3,800 Western Division locomotives were allocated to Crewe for repairs and it is this number which could not be repainted — and this undoubtedly led to this story being told.

William A. Stanier arrived on the LMS in 1932, bringing with him a strong personal interest in machine tools and modern works practices, together with an insistence to achieve much finer precision and quality of

finish, especially for axle boxes and axle journals. Combined with a new design of axlebox this new outlook considerably reduced the number of 'hot boxes' so that this problem was no longer a consideration in a considerable number of new larger locomotives which were now part of the Company's stock.

World War II saw a different effort from Crewe, compared with that of 1914-18. During the 1939-45 conflict a much smaller effort was diverted to armaments because the Government had placed a higher priority upon the need to keep locomotives in good running order. By 1942 the production of armaments had virtually ceased, with work being concentrated upon locomotive affairs, both early LMS and Stanier type together with American 2–8–0s making them fit for service overseas and in the UK.

On January 1 1948 the LMS handed over to British Railways a very efficient Works and its allocation of locomotives for general repairs was made up of more than 2,500 steam locomotives. The Works is still in existence and, at the time of writing is still the largest works associated with BR, handling major repairs to electric and diesel electric locomotives and employing around 4,000 men.

In the pictures that follow we are able to see what was happening in the Works during three separate photographic visits. Unless otherwise mentioned all these views were taken in September 1934 when a publicity visit was arranged around the theme of the 1935 building programme, for which 117 new locomotives had been

Left: The staying operation in progress. Using a pneumatic tool, a pair of works staff are screwing copper stays through the steel firebox wrapper plate and into the copper firebox within, holding it firmly in position. The threaded ends can be seen on the stays nearest the camera: the plain centre section will eventually lie within the water space between copper firebox and steel wrapper. Once screwed into position, the stays will be rivetted over.

Below: This must have been an awful job: rivetters are at work on the throat plate and firebox sides of an unidentified boiler. It must have been utterly deafening to work in these circumstances and unlike today, no ear defenders are being used by these men, who seem content in their cloth caps. The size of the water space between copper firebox and steel wrapper plate is clearly indicated by the width of the foundation ring, which closes the gap at its lower edge. The holes drilled and tapped in the foundation ring will carry the ashpan mounting studs.

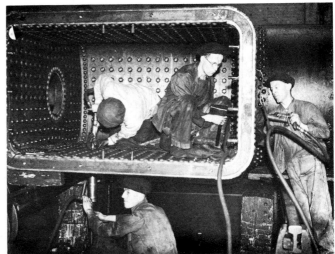

Left: The boiler of a new 'Jubilee' class 5XP 4–6–0 is lowered into the main frames at Crewe on September 14 1934. The hole in the base of the smokebox through which the blast-pipe will pass is clearly visible, as are the lower parts of the firebox and the ashpan, which are normally invisible. Note that the boiler cladding plates have already been fitted — apart from where the lifting slings are positioned — and that wheeling is the last job carried out in engine building and repair.

ordered. At the time of the visit it was suggested by the caption writers that the Works was turning out out two new locomotives a week and while Crewe was certainly capable of such an achievement, it is quite likely that a degree of journalistic licence was used by the press when the story was projected. Some views were taken a little earlier in 1931, and from the press captions it is difficult to find a specific reason for the visit, unlike the third date when the theme was 'The making of a Streamliner', a photographic assignment carried out by 'Picture Post' magazine.

Right: A new 'Jubilee' 4–6–0 takes shape at Crewe, on September 14 1934. The boiler has been fitted to the frames and the leading four-wheel bogie is apparently ready to roll into position. Note the end of the inside cylinder's steam chest, visible beneath the smokebox. The end cover has yet to be fitted on the ring of studs

Below: A Stanier taper boiler receives its steam fittings and asbestos insulation at Crewe, prior to fitting in the frames. This was long before the health dangers associated with asbestos were appreciated — and look how young the chap on the right appears to be! The 'No.5277' painted on the boiler barrel just ahead of the firebox indicates that this was destined for a 'Black 5' which entered traffic in December 1936. The handrail brackets along the boiler side are visible, as are the brackets on the firebox sides which will support the boiler on the rear of the main frames. The asbestos was mixed with water and applied in paste form, and note the studs, screwed into the foundation ring, on which the ashpan will be mounted. and part of the valve-setting equipment is attached to the spindle.

Right: A splendid view of the Crewe works paintshop in September 1934, with 'Jubilee' 4–6–0 No.5625 the centre of attention. No.5625, which entered service in October 1934, was nameless until 1936, when it became *Sarawak*, one of many 'Jubilees' to receive 'Empire' names as part of the policy adopted by the LMS to commemorate the Jubilee year of King George V in 1936. The naming policy started with the Dominions and proceeded through the Colonies before moving onto famous Naval Admirals and the battles they fought, although a scientist — Lord Rutherford of Nelson — was included in this batch. The naming series then embraced famous warships of the past, together with a few contemporary examples before ending with a batch of pioneer engine names, and a few with Irish connections. Barely in view in this picture on the left is No.5624, which in 1936 was named *St Helena*. The LMS painting schedule for red engines in 1935 allowed five days for painting and lining, plus varnish hardening time

Above: This impressive and evocative publicity picture was taken on December 9 1936, and depicts five brand new 'Jubilee' 4–6–0s, Nos.5734–38, *Meteor, Comet, Phoenix, Atlas* and *Samson* — probably the first and last time they were side-by-side in this manner! The picture was one of a series produced to reinforce the claim that the LMS was putting six new locomotives into service each week at this time.

Above: An attractive view of No.5736 *Phoenix*, also on December 9 1936, undergoing steam test prior to introduction into service. This is a picture of interest, for not only does it give a clear view of the locomotive's crosshead-driven vacuum exhauster, but it also shows No.5736 in its original form. This locomotive, together with sister engine 5735 *Comet*, was rebuilt in 1942 (as part of Stanier's last major locomotive design work for the LMS) with a higher-pressure Type 2A taper boiler and double exhaust. The pair were subsequently reclassified 6P (equal to the unrebuilt 'Royal Scot' 4–6–0s) and their performance led directly to the order being given for the rebuilding of a second batch of 10 'Royal Scot' engines with the 2A boiler. *Phoenix* was withdrawn by BR in September 1964 as No.45736, and was scrapped by Hughes Bolckows Ltd, North Blyth, in January 1965, after a period in store Carlisle Kingmoor shed.

BUILDING THE 'STREAMLINERS'

IN 1937, 'Picture Post' magazine took its imaginative photographic approach inside Crewe Works to depict the construction of Stanier's magnificent 'Princess Coronation' class streamlined 'Pacifics'. The photographer did an excellent job and produced a fascinating series of photographs, but Picture Post story 393 was never published, and the file prints at the BBC Hulton Picture Library all carry the description 'story killed'. Many of these highly evocative photographs are consequently published here for the first time.

Above: The story starts in the Crewe Works forge, where all reciprocating motion parts were made, and here a group of men are skilfully forging a connecting rod. The white-hot steel billet, which emerged from the furnace as a short, squat ingot, is being literally pounded into shape by the massive 30-ton steam hammer. The men either side of the hammer head are using 'setting-down tools' whilst a third man holds a 'stopper' in position to direct the force of the impact to shape the small end. The forge crew was expected to use a billet which contained precisely the correct amount of steel to fashion the required item — any waste which had to be cut away and discarded, was frowned upon.

Right: Another piece of motion is shaped in the forge. The hammer head has just struck and the 'stopper' is in position alongside the glowing billet to determine the height of the finished connecting rod. The white-capped man on the right is the 'main hammer man', who supervised the operation and used a complex series of nods and other signals to instruct the 'hammer driver' (on the right, wearing a cloth cap) to drop the hammer head with varying degrees of force during the forging operation. Working the hammer was not an all-or-nothing affair, and a wide range of blows from a featherweight 'tap' to the full 30-ton impact were available.

Left: A pair of connecting rod forgings are fluted on a horizontal milling machine, on which the spinning milling cutters remain stationary, whilst the bed on which the rods are secured moves horizontally beneath them. The cutters are being kept cool by a constant flow of an oil/water emulsion which drained through the machine into a sump, where it was filtered and pumped away for re-use. What will eventually be the big ends of this pair of rods are nearest the camera.

Below: The finishing touches are put to a pair of connecting rods which have been fluted, machined, bored, fitted with brass bushes and provided with their oil reservoirs since they were battered into shape in the forge. These men are filing the edges of a finished pair of standard rods for 'Jubilee' or class 5 4–6–0 types. In the background a machine operator has a similar rod mounted on a vertical borer, which is drilling out the big and small ends simultaneously, after which the brass bushes will be pressed into position and bored-out to size. On his right, a vertical slotter is being used to prepare axleboxes for the pressing-in of their brasses.

Right: A 1937 view inside the Crewe Works 'smithy', as a very well-built blacksmith pauses from his labours. Definitely not a gentleman to argue with!

Below: It is recorded that the first locomotive frames were 'hacked out' using hammers and chisels: by 1937 much more sophisticated methods were in use and here the main frames of a locomotive are being cut from steel plate using a template (left) to guide the oxycoalgas cutters. This pair of men have just started a new set of frames, and the operator nearest the camera has just completed cutting an axlebox slot. This operation was subsequently automated.

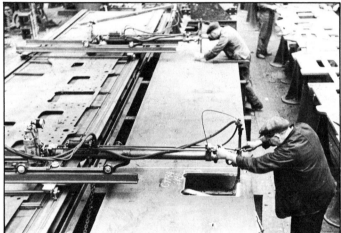

Above, right: The complex flanged firebox plates were produced by heating the steel plate and then squeezing it to shape between shaped blocks in an enormous press, and here a firebox throatplate, still glowing white-hot, is being lifted from the lower flanging block by an overhead crane, following removal from the press in the background. Note how the plate has been secured on the twin 'spikes' on the right hand edge of the flanging block: this was done to prevent the steel plate being squeezed out of position as the upper flanging block made contact in the press.

Right: Having already been shaped in the press, this plate clearly needed further detailed attention, and here it is being re-heated in the furnace. Note the sand floor and the locomotive fire-irons stood on the right of the door.

Right: With re-heating complete and the glowing steel plate replaced on the flanging block, heavy wooden malletts are being used with vigour to beat one corner firmly into shape. The heat in this workshop was intense, yet the only protection these men are wearing are cloth caps pulled down to shield the eyes. Many men suffered eye problems — including blindness in later life, in severe cases — as a result of working in conditions like these for many years.

Left: A new steel driving wheel tyre is heated using an enormous adjustable gas ring sunk into the wheelshop floor. When the tyre is sufficiently expanded, the driving wheel will be lowered into position and the gas switched off, the tyre shrinking tightly in place. The upper wheel of this set has already been tyred and the axle journals polished where they will sit in the axlebox brasses. A selection of other wheels are awaiting their tyres, whilst further down the shop, a crank axle from a four-cylinder locomotive is being moved by an overhead crane.

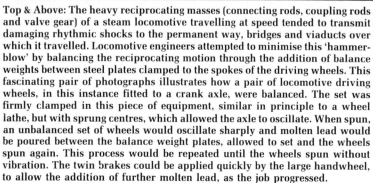

Top & Above: The heavy reciprocating masses (connecting rods, coupling rods and valve gear) of a steam locomotive travelling at speed tended to transmit damaging rhythmic shocks to the permanent way, bridges and viaducts over which it travelled. Locomotive engineers attempted to minimise this 'hammer-blow' by balancing the reciprocating motion through the addition of balance weights between steel plates clamped to the spokes of the driving wheels. This fascinating pair of photographs illustrates how a pair of locomotive driving wheels, in this instance fitted to a crank axle, were balanced. The set was firmly clamped in this piece of equipment, similar in principle to a wheel lathe, but with sprung centres, which allowed the axle to oscillate. When spun, an unbalanced set of wheels would oscillate sharply and molten lead would be poured between the balance weight plates, allowed to set and the wheels spun again. This process would be repeated until the wheels spun without vibration. The twin brakes could be applied quickly by the large handwheel, to allow the addition of further molten lead, as the job progressed.

Left: Brand new, gleaming brass fittings are mounted on a 'Pacific' boiler, prior to the application of asbestos lagging and steel cladding plates. The fitter is mounting the 'sand gun', which fired a jet of steam and sand at the firebox tubeplate, and was designed to remove encrusted soot, which might block the tubes and thus impair steaming. This device was subsequently discontinued, as over-use caused extensive erosive damage to copper tubeplates, which were very expensive to repair or replace.

Below: This Stanier 'Pacific' boiler is almost ready to be lowered into the main frames: the cladding is complete, firehole doors and boiler fittings are all in place and the hopper ashpan is being attached to the firebox foundation ring. Below the main manifold at the top of the backplate can be seen the twin water gauge glasses and the steam valves for the injectors, while beneath the regulator handle can be seen the handle of the blower and the wheel-operated valve of the sand gun. On the left, the driver's brake valve and steam sanding valve are surmounted by the vacuum ejector control valves. LNWR 'Super D' 0—8—0 No.9078 is alongside.

Left: In the Crewe boiler shop, a 'Pacific' boiler has been suspended from an overhead crane whilst rivetting is in progress. The rivets are being heated to the correct temperature in the mobile unit in the foreground. Powered by electricity, the cold rivets were fitted between two electrodes and heated in the same way as the bar of an electric fire, and two rivets can be seen ready for use. An apprentice stands ready with a pair of tongs to pass the white-hot rivets to the skilled man supervising the work. Note the deep pits into which boilers could be lowered, so that all rivetting could be done from ground level.

Right, above: A 'Princess Coronation' boiler has been completed and lagged, and is being paired with its new frames for the first time — and the engine really begins to take shape. Note the sloping top of the smokebox, in place of the normal, cylindrical pattern, needed because of the streamlined nose. When de-streamlined, this unusual feature was most evident and remained until new smokeboxes were fitted during subsequent works visits. The boiler is perfectly balanced on a single crane hook as it is lowered into the frames. The boiler cladding is complete, apart from the section of barrel in front of the firebox where the steel lifting cables are placed, and note the twin 'cut-outs' in the cladding plates, provided to enable the mechanical lubricator lids to be opened.

Right, below: The sleek, streamlined image of the 'Princess Coronation' class depended on a very neat external appearance, and highly skilled sheet metalwork was needed to ensure that the outer casing which covered the smokebox door closed correctly. A fitter is at work here on a streamlined nose, making sure all will be in order at a later stage.

Left: A fascinating photograph which reveals how the leading bogie located in the frames of a 'Princess Coronation' class 'Pacific'. A pair of semi-spherical protrusions on the underside of the locomotive located in the cups positioned on each side of the bogie frame — one of which is visible immediately in front of the man on the right — while the enormous central pin provided an anchorage and pivot. The locomotive visible in the background is an unidentified Stanier 2–6–4T, painted in the 1936 block-style livery.

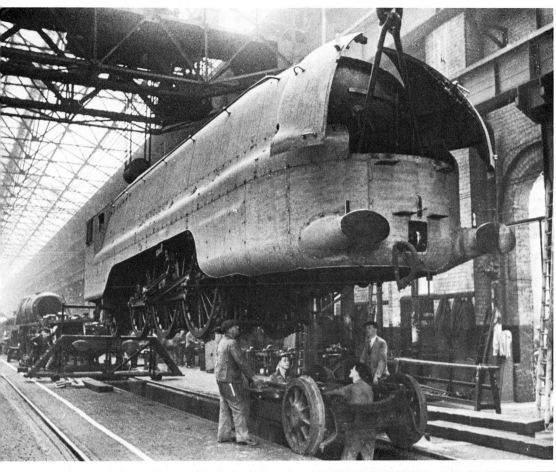

Left: An impressive sight indeed as a virtually completed 'Princess Coronation' is gently lowered onto its leading bogie in the erecting shop (see also facing page, bottom). The conventional smokebox door, normally concealed behind the smooth nose is visible, and note also the recessed drawhook. From here the locomotive would be coupled to its tender and despatched to the paintshop.

Below: An unidentified 'City' member of the 'Princess Coronation' class is the subject of attention in the Crewe works paintshop, in 1937. The job is almost complete and the original caption proclaims: "the engine ... will soon be ready to take its place in public service with nearly 8,000 other LMS locomotives. One thousand men have laboured to produce it, but only a hand picked dozen or so will have the thrill of driving it."

DERBY WORKS

WE now turn to look at the Derby locomotive works, built by the Midland Railway, which as a Company had adopted a different approach to stock building, as compared with the LNWR. As a general rule, the 'Premier Line' had constructed its coaches at Wolverton, wagons at Earlestown and locomotives at Crewe. Very little had come from outside builders and as far as locomotives were concerned, only a handful had been 'bought in' between 1919 and 1921, to ease the post-war shortage.

The MR had adopted a different philosophy. All home-built locomotives and carriages were built at Derby, but in the 19th century the MR had employed the great independent locomotive builders to a great extent and at the time of the Grouping Derby lagged behind Crewe in terms of capacity. Nevertheless, the MR's 20th century needs had been largely met by Derby, and the works scored marginally over Crewe in the respect that its roots were older: part of the Derby works site had been bought as early as 1838 and by 1840 the offices and workshops of the North Midland Railway Company (one of the three constituents of the MR at its formation in 1844) were operative.

This section depicts three press visits to the works at Derby and these pictures are placed in chronological order. The emphasis on the February 23 1926 visit was the quantity of engines being turned out by the works.

Right: In this picture, a boiler is being held vertically whilst hydraulic rivetting takes place, securing the barrel sections together. The boiler tubes and copper firebox have yet to be fitted, and note the strengthening 'patches' around the 'mudhole' doors on the top corners of the firebox. The shop floor is provided with a deep pit, into which the boiler could be lowered, to facilitate rivetting of any part of the barrel or firebox. Note the pile of coal on the right, needed for the furnace used to heat rivets.

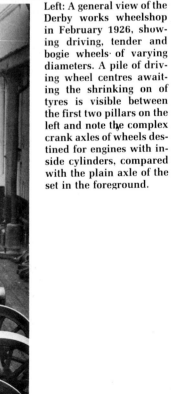

Left: A general view of the Derby works wheelshop in February 1926, showing driving, tender and bogie wheels of varying diameters. A pile of driving wheel centres awaiting the shrinking on of tyres is visible between the first two pillars on the left and note the complex crank axles of wheels destined for engines with inside cylinders, compared with the plain axle of the set in the foreground.

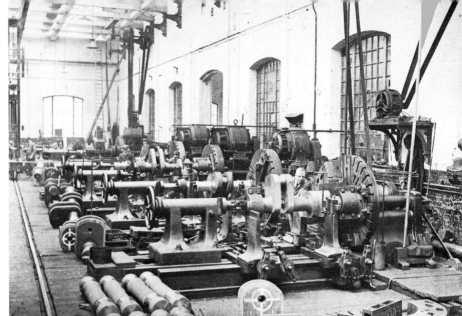

Right: A machine shop in which axles are prepared for fitting to their wheels. Crank axles are being machined in the first three lathes, whilst further examples are lying on the floor, awaiting attention. Part of a crank axle in the centre foreground is marked ready for boring-out, as is the crank of the axle on the left of the second lathe. A number of plain axles are also lying on the shop floor in the foreground.

Left: Adjacent to the boiler shop at Derby was the brass foundry and a tilting furnace is being used to pour molten brass into the carrier from which it will be poured into the moulds during the casting of non-ferrous parts. Brass castings would be machined in the neighbouring brass fitting shop. This foundryman is wearing a very sturdy pair of wooden-soled clogs!

Left, below: In the boiler shop large hammers are being used to thin the corners of a flanged firebox throat plate, the double row of staggered holes along the lower edge will be used to rivet the firebox to the foundation ring, whilst the other holes will carry stays to secure the firebox. The centrally-placed oval pattern of holes drilled to the left of the foundation ring rivet holes will be cut-out to form a hand-hole, used to remove accumulated scale during boiler washing.

Left: A completed boiler is prepared for fitting to a locomotive chassis. The boiler is almost certainly a G7 S type, for one of the class 4 0–6–0s which were under construction at Derby in 1926. Rivetting and stay detail are clearly shown, as are the 'handholes' on the top edge of the firebox, and the sharp slope of the grate.

Right: An excellent view of the 30-ton steam hammer in the Derby works forge, also in 1926. Various axles and motion parts are in the foreground, awaiting machining. The hammer is being used in this picture to shape what appears to be a big end strap. Supervising operations is the 'main hammer man' (in the white hat) whilst the 'hammer driver' is on the left.

Right: In this final February 1926 picture a class 4 4–4–0 (later class 4P) 'Compound' locomotive is being lowered onto its wheels in the erecting shop, alongside a new class 4 0–6–0 which is being erected on the next road. Note the axleboxes and springs, already assembled on the axle, ready to slip into the horns on the main frame as the engine is lowered into position.

Left: An almost surreal view at Derby on January 22 1935, showing a vast quantity of wheels, mainly for coaches. Note the pressed-steel wheels, identifiable by the holes in the disc, and the older Mansell wheels, with their securing rims. A spoked wagon wheel is just visible in the bottom right corner.

CIVIL ENGINEERING

MAINTAINING the extensive LMS system in good order was a never-ending task for the Company's civil engineers. In many cases, repairs and new construction had to be carried out whilst trains continued to run, and this need to keep routes open whilst work was carried out to bridges and other structures, or to close them for only minimal periods periods caused for a high degree of organisation and planning from the civil engineers. The replacement of bridges — usually carried out overnight — called for much careful work with the new bridge being built alongside the life-expired structure, which was then rolled out sideways on channels of ball bearings and the new bridge rolled in by the same method. These pictures give an idea of some of the tasks required of the civil engineers.

Above: How to insert a new road underbridge into a section of plain embankment. On June 24 1934 LMS civil engineers were making final preparations for the installation of a bridge to carry the railway over a new road at School Lane, between East Didsbury and Burnage stations, in Manchester. This view shows how wooden shuttering had been built through the embankment to allow bricklayers to construct the bridge retaining and wing walls, and abutments. The new steel bridge has been constructed on a temporary decking on the far side of the track, and is almost ready to be rolled into position. The new roadway, pavements and street lights are all ready for use. Once the bridge has been installed the former embankment beneath will be excavated to complete the road link.

Left: An elevated view giving a clear view of how the new 160-ton bridge in Manchester was constructed on-site, adjacent to its final position. All preparations are complete: the retaining/wing walls and abutments are ready, the track lifted and engineers are preparing to roll the bridge into place. The installation was completed overnight, and the railway reopened within 12 hours.

Left: When bridges were replaced as illustrated on page 130, the new structures were rolled into position from their temporary decking on channels of ball-bearings. This picture depicts the technique in action on January 14 1934 as a new bridge is prepared for installation at Harlesden, in North London. The new 215-ton bridge had been built to replace an older structure which carried the Cricklewood—Acton line over Acton Lane.

Below: A pair of massive girders required for a track-widening operation at Thornes Road, between Horbury and Wakefield, in Yorkshire, arrive on site in the charge of a Fowler '4F' 0–6–0. The brake vans are of LNWR origin whilst the girders were carried on a pair of brand new 50-ton standard twin girder trucks, built to Lot 298, and carrying running numbers 263369/20 and 269943/9. Their details were recorded on page 137 of the LMS Special Wagon Diagram Book.

Left: A pair of steam cranes lower one of the Thornes Road girders (seen above) onto a pair of small bogies, on which it will be rolled sideways on the temporary rails laid along the retaining walls, to its final position. Note the track clamps beneath the crane's buffers, which in conjunction with the outriggers, stabilised the crane during heavy lifting operations.

Above: A major engineering feat carried out in 1925 was the opening-up of Chevet Tunnel, between Chevet and Shydale, in Yorkshire. Built by Robert Stephenson, this 720-yard tunnel was opened for traffic by the North Midland Railway in May 1840. In 1844, the NMR became part of the Midland Railway and this double-track section became a troublesome bottle-neck. This March 1925 view shows excavation work in progress using a variety of equipment. By opening out the tunnel it became possible to lay a four-track section through a deep cutting, whose highest point was almost 100ft above track level. This picture clearly illustrates the massive amount of spoil which had to be excavated and removed.

Right: Another major widening took place in the Birmingham area in 1929 with the opening-up of Cofton Tunnel, near Barnt Green, on the New Street—Gloucester line. The tunnel was opened using explosives and on January 29 1929 rubble is being cleared following a recent blast.

Left: In order to enable the new Stanier 4–6–0s of class 5 and 5XP to run over the Derby—Manchester section it was necessary to undertake a programme of bridge strengthening. On February 28 1935 reconstruction work is underway at Burleigh bridge, near Derby. Traffic continued to run whilst workmen sank supports for the new bridge alongside, and here 'Compound' 4–4–0 No.1045, the first of the LMS standard 'Compounds', as distinct from the earlier MR locomotives, steams past. Built at Derby in 1924, No.1045 survived until 1957 when it was withdrawn as British Railways No.41045. Unlike the MR-built engines, which were fitted with 7ft diameter driving wheels, No.1045 and her LMS sisters ran with 6ft 9in driving wheels. Unlike the later LMS-built 'Compounds', which placed the driver on the left-hand side of the cab, No.1045 was a right-hand drive locomotive. Finally, note that the engine is fitted with a tall Stanier chimney.

Right: A new road under-bridge takes shape on June 19 1932, between Thorpe Bay and South-end on the LT&S Section of the LMS. The new railway bridge is complete and in position and the road beneath is being excavated using a narrow gauge wagonway. Wooden shuttering is in position to enable the construction of bridge abutments and the retaining/wing walls.

Above: '3P' 4–4–2T No.2155 hauls the first train over the new bridge between Thorpe Bay and Southend (see page 133, bottom). Work had continued through the night rolling the new bridge into position, under the interested gaze of a large crowd of holiday makers. No.2155 was one of the final batch of locomotives built by the LMS to the LTSR design. Completed in 1930 it became No.1973 in 1947, but the number was never actually carried. British Railways added 40000 to the number at Nationalisation, the locomotive becoming No.41973. It survived until withdrawal in 1955: the last of these LMS-built 4–4–2Ts was withdrawn in 1960.

Right: All bridges and civil engineering structures need continuous care and attention if they are to remain in good condition, and here a gang of 23 painters are at work repainting Arnside viaduct, on the Furness line, between Carnforth and Ulverston. The task took six months to complete, and the gang tied lifebelts to the viaduct on the downstream side, in case anyone fell into the River Kent estuary, which is tidal at this point.

Left: The changes in economic circumstances in the 1920s and 1930s, together with the increasing cost of labour, caused the 'Big Four' railway companies to rethink many of their traditional methods, in a drive to become cost effective. In this view we see how the LMS tackled the problem of killing weeds, which choked the ballast and could impair drainage. The 1930s solution was to produce the weed killing train, though there were variations between the systems used by the main line companies. The LMS, unlike the other three companies, mixed the chemical and water together before spraying, though along with the LNER and SR, the LMS used a simple geared axle drive, unlike the GWR, which employed steam to pump the mixture from the tanks into the spray heads. The train in this picture is being hauled by an unidentified LNWR 4–4–0 of either the 'George the Fifth' or 'Precursor' class. Two 10-ton Midland Railway Brake vans converted for spraying are at each end of the train, which comprises two LNWR tenders of Bowen-Cooke design converted to carry the weedkilling mixture. In this view the equipment is in the spraying position and the 5/34 painting date, just beneath the roof of the brake van, provides a clue to when this picture was taken, while at work on the Western Division, near Rugby.

ROAD VEHICLES

THE LMS was, in its day, a very large operator of a wide range of road vehicles of both horse-drawn and powered types. These pictures do not provide comprehensive coverage of the LMS road fleet, but they give an idea of the LMS approach to this interesting aspect of railway operation in the inter-war years.

Above: The mechanical horse was developed by the LMS at Wolverton and was introduced to the press and into service in 1931. On No.2G, hydraulic arms picked up the front axle of a horse cart and deposited it onto carrying brackets on the tractor chassis. Subsequent mechanical horses used ramp-style couplings by Wolverton, Karrier, or Scammell. The tractor is a Karrier 'Cob' unit, which was designed for refuse collection in narrow alleyways. When Wolverton combined this unit with a rapidly-coupled semi-trailer it proved to be a most economical and manouverable piece of road transport. No.2G must have been difficult for the driver with its solid tyres and open-sided cab. There were no trailer brakes, and only the rear tractor wheels had brakes. Driving the tractor must have been very uncomfortable on a wet day, bouncing and slithering on cobblestones and granite sets.

Right: This Rolls Royce promotions van was one of the Company's more exotic road vehicles! The majority of the public only travelled by train for perhaps one return journey per year, during their annual holiday. In order to induce more people to travel more often — and greater distances — by train, either of which would produce a desirable increase in revenue, the promotion of leisure travel became a major feature of railway advertising. In conjunction with the holiday resorts, brochures were produced by the LMS for general distribution, together with railway travel pamphlets for distribution within specific areas. This provided the travelling public with ideas for new holiday venues, together with the means of reaching them. Travel agents were not common at this time and anyone needing this information had to visit their nearest railway station, and in an attempt to put the advertising leaflets into local High Streets and other public places, the LMS purchased a second-hand Rolls Royce and fitted it with a combination display case/library body. This opulent vehicle, complete with its smartly liveried attendant, toured town centres dispensing holiday literature — and it proved to be a very effective advertising medium. The vehicle was then moved on to another area, frequently by train.

TO reinforce the advertising campaign instituted by the Rolls Royce vehicle, a variety of lesser vehicles were converted for publicity purposes, ranging from converted horse carts to service-expired motor vehicles. This example. No.NK 4618 (fleet No.30D) is a Ford-T chassis with LMS-built bodywork, built at Wolverton, probably constructed as a continuation of an LNWR Lot. The Ford radiator badge has been obscured by a plate with raised LMS letters, a practice which enjoyed some popularity in the earlier days. The 'D' suffix to the number indicates that it had originally been used as a parcels van and as such was finished in the more elaborate lake and black livery with coach-style lettering. As an advertising unit it has been specially prepared to the extent of removing the enamel from the radiator and polishing the exposed metal. The big white placard on the side is the only major conversion for its advertising duties. It proclaims: "This car carries Beautifully Illustrated Guides and Programmes of Tourist and Excursion Bookings to UNRIVALLED HOLIDAY RESORTS on the Company's System." Internally, it was probably fitted with racks to hold pamphlets and the van probably carried a portable stall for use at fêtes and other special events. It is pictured on the Embankment, in London.

Above: Together with the other Railways, the LMS started to develop container traffic as a major transport system in 1929. To promote the system, several series of photographs were taken showing various traffics conveyed by container. In most cases, the road vehicle involved is one of these AEC chassis, fitted with a cab and dray at Wolverton. The cab is a nationally standard product and is offset to the offside as necessary to accommodate driving controls. Judging by the registration number, the chassis is comparatively new although the style of the radiator bonnet and wings is very dated for the era (probably 1930). The dray was also a standard product, anchored to the chassis by U-bolts. This enabled the drays to be changed over rapidly in the event of damage or should a change of body be required for other traffic needs. Besides container traffic, the lorry would also be available for general loads and carried its own weather-sheet on the cab roof. The cab only has half-doors, but there is electric lighting and a full windscreen. The chassis and cab have one fleet number with a 'B' suffix (930–B) and the dray has another fleet number, as benefits an interchangeable unit. This vehicle was being used as part of the LMS furniture removal service.

Right: To promote its containerised furniture removal service, the LMS staged this demonstration, where a furniture container has been lifted aboard one of the Company's lorries, registration number UR 8882. The crane is one of several owned by the LMS for handling containers, and had been developed jointly by the Company and general engineers Walkers, of Wigan. The crane could luff, traverse and travel while supporting a loaded container

(about six tons dead weight) and the driver could control the vehicle facing either way. The chassis was by Pagefield, Walker's lorry division, and it was fitted with solid tyres. The 'X' suffix to its number (42) indicates that the crane was for internal use only and was not registered for use on a public road. With each crane the Pagefield company supplied a small four-wheeled trailer, which carried a second set of wheels fitted with pneumatic tyres. When the crane needed to travel on public roads the solid tyred wheels (essential for stability when the crane was used for heavy lifting in the LMS

yards) were removed and the pneumatic tyres fitted for easier travel. As an unregistered vehicle, journeys from yard to yard by these cranes were probably undertaken on 'trade plates' but certain types of plant travelling only a limited distance on public highways were exempt from road tax and it is possible that these vehicles qualified for this exemption. Little can be said about the lorry, apart from the fact that the bodywork was built at Wolverton, and in common with nearly all the railway heavy lorries, the container overhung the rear edge of the dray.

Right: A corner of the goods yard at St Pancras in April 1926, during a lightning strike by carting staff in the period befoe the commencement of the general strike one month later. Most of the horse vehicles are sheeted over, but the presence of horses and men would suggest that they were returning to the yard with loads collected from traders, perhaps bewildered at finding the yard idle. Cart No.2670 (foreground) is a former Midland Type 12, built to carry three tons, whilst No.316 (middle distance, right) is a Type 10, still carrying its Midland Railway Company lettering. No.2670 has a single tilt frame with canopy to give the carter some shelter in poor weather. From this frame a tarpaulin could also be hung to cover the load. Most of the sheeted-over vehicles also appear to be Types 10 and 12, although on either side of the yard cabin there are flat drays: No.2646 just visible to the right is a type 22, whilst to the left there is a stand dray with removable flat. The yard cabin is constructed from standard Midland Railway signal box parts. There is much detail here of use to the railway modeller seeking to create the whole railway scene rather than just its locomotives and trains.

FOR local door-to-door deliveries and collections of packages, horse transport remained economically viable well beyond the demise of the LMS. Indeed, horses would probably still be viable in terms of 'running costs', but the inconvenience of having to attend to them during weekends, holidays and strikes creates a high inconvenience factor. This delightful picture shows a company horse parcels van and crew making a delivery. The driver has collected the packages while the blinkered horse waits patiently. The van boy, whose job was to aid the driver on intensive traffic routes, stands on the tailboard holding on to a knotted rope, which was an important fitting. Officially it was provided as a hand-hold to aid mounting and dismounting of the rather high tailboard. Unofficially, it provided the boy with something to hang on to when travelling about on the tailboard, which was his usual travelling position. The rear curtains are neatly rolled and tied, which was unusual, as they were usually unrolled to protect the load from the weather. All parcels vans (horse and motor) had advertising panels on both sides of the tilt, and it was rare to see one without a poster. The horse is a comparatively light animal and with this steel-tyred van it could probably sustain a trot on a good surface for a respectable distance. Some stations with steep approaches kept a boy and trace horse on duty to couple on and act as a 'pilot engine' up the bank, when heavy loads were being hauled.

PEOPLE AND SPECIAL EVENTS

Above: LMS Chairman Sir Josiah Stamp in his office, at 10.33am on February 1 1937. This homely and very cosy office is very different indeed from the type of office in which his 1986 equivalent would work! A model of one of Stanier's pioneer 'Pacifics' is on the mantlepiece and an enormous fire is roaring in the grate! Sir Josiah Stamp became a Peer in the King's Birthday Honours of 1938, taking the title Baron Stamp of Shortlands. He was killed, at the age of 61 years, together with his wife and eldest son, on April 17 1941, when their home in Beckenham received a direct hit by a German bomb.

JOSIAH CHARLES STAMP was born on June 21 1880. Joining the Civil Service in 1896, he is recorded as being a conscientious hard worker who never stopped working. He took a First Class degree in Economics and Political Science in 1911; he was a Cobder Prizeman in 1912 and D Sc in 1916 and a Hutchinson Research medallist in the same year. As a Council member of the Royal Statistical Society in 1916 he was to progress, becoming its joint Secretary then Editor of its 'Proceedings' and finally its President in 1930-32 thereafter an Honorary Vice President. In addition, he became a Council Member of the Royal Economic Society in 1920. During World War I he became involved with industry and business when he administered the Excess Profits Duty and this lead to him leaving Government to become a Director and Secretary of Nobel Industries Ltd, which was to become part of a new enterprise, Imperial Chemical Industries, now better known as ICI.

Becoming a CBE in 1918, a KBE in 1920 and a GBE in 1924, the same year as he was a British Representative on the Reparations Commission's 1924 Committee on German Currency and Finance, which itself initiated the formation of the German State Railways. This was the background of the man who was to head the LMS.

In 1925 the LMS Board announced the creation of a new office, that of President of the Executive. Executive Control was to be vested in the President with four Vice Presidents to form an Executive Committee and they were to be assisted by a Secretary and a Chief Legal Adviser. Stamp took office in January 1926 and the scene was set for the formation of this new executive which, in addition to Stamp as President, comprised J. H. Follows CBE for Railway Traffic (operating and Commercial) Section. S. H. Hunt CBE for the same function, J. Quirey MI Inst T, for Accounting and Service Departments and R. W. Reid MI MECH E for Works and Ancillary undertakings. The backgrounds of these Vice Presidents were, Follows (Midland Railway), Hunt (LNWR) while Reid was also from the Midland

Left: This photograph, taken on July 12 1938, illustrates LMS Chairman Lord Stamp pressing a button in his Euston office which detonated a huge explosion at Caldon Low Quarries, near Leek, Staffordshire, 150 miles away. The original caption records that a considerable amount of stone produced by the blast would be used by the company during the rebuilding of Euston, as described in Chapter 1.

Railway which thereby ensured that a strong Derby influence would exist in the upper echelons of the Company.

Sir Josiah Stamp was described as a puritan who at the most would only drink fizzy water but who had fresh ideas and a formidable intellect. One of his most successful ploys was to arrange matters so that first he cleared the way by promoting the CME Sir Henry Fowler to become a Vice President of the Company and then in his place promoting Ernest Lemon. However, Lemon was another Midland man and his considerable administrative talents qualified him for a higher post and so he too became a Vice President of the LMS, thus leaving the field open for an outsider to be appointed CME, and thereby avoiding the problem of appointing an 'insider' who would inevitably have strong loyalties to his own pre-Grouping company and its methods.

Stamp's choice for CME was William Stanier, who had already served the Great Western Railway for almost 40 years. Lunched by Stamp, Lemon and Sir Harold Hartley (another Vice President) it was put to Stanier that he might consider being the CME of the greatest railway company in the world and in due course he accepted the post with a cordial blessing from the Great Western Railway.

During the years Stamp was President of the LMS he strove to improve the efficiency of the company and in some ways had a touch of Beeching and Thatcher about him — although the results of his work were not so evident in closures or the reduction of overmanning. Truly the railways were overmanned in the LMS era and regrettably it never managed to successfully get to grips with the problem.

Stamp's death came on April 16 1941 when a direct hit by a bomb on his home killed the First Baron Stamp of Shortlands, his lady and eldest son; they were three more casualties of Hitler's War. He was succeeded as President by his senior Vice President William Valentine Wood, an Ulster-

Above: Military namings frequently justified parades, and here we see the unveiling of a regimental crest, on a locomotive which was already named. 'Royal Scot' 4–6–0 No.6112 was built by the North British Locomotive Company in 1927 and named *Sherwood Forester* in the following year. In this photograph, dated June 16 1933, we see Major R.L. Sherbrook and the Mayor of Derby, at Derby Works, preparing to unveil the regimental crest, which was a gift of the regiment to the LMS. On parade are members of the regiment, together with interested LMS employees, while in the background are a number of locomotives of which only 4–4–0 class 3P No.712 can be identified. No.6112 was fitted with a type 2A taper boiler and double-chimney in 1943, and was withdrawn from service in 1964 as BR No.46112. No.712 was withdrawn at the end of 1938.

man whose railway career began on the Belfast and Northern Counties Railway in 1898.

This chapter looks at the activities of Stamp, together with a few special events.

Right: The original caption to this picture, entitled, 'Human Shuttlecocks' and dated August 21 1925, was about two brothers working for the LMS who frequently passed each other, but never met. William Dean, shown here, and his brother Harry were restaurant car conductors on the 'Irish Mail' services running between Euston and Holyhead and it was claimed that they had not seen each other for 16 years! With both trains running to time Harry and William were likely to pass each other near Colwyn Bay — or so the story goes! Whatever the truth of the story — which probably appeared during a 'slow' news period — the picture reveals fascinating detail about the Company uniform of this period.

Left: Produced by a Topical Press Agency photographer during a spell of hot weather, this marvellous picture was entitled 'A welcome refreshment for the engine driver' — no mention of his fireman! Two young ladies in summer dresses of the period are handing cold drinks (complete with straws!) to the footplate crew aboard 'Patriot' 4–6–0 No.5519 *Lady Godiva*, as they await to depart from Euston. Built at Crewe in 1933 as No.6008, this engine was renumbered 5519 in 1934. This locomotive was not one of the 'Patriots' subsequently rebuilt with a Type 2A taper boiler, and it was withdrawn in original condition by British Railways, as No.45519, in March 1962. It was scrapped at Crewe in the same month.

Left: An interesting motive power comparison during the 1930 centenary celebrations, as 0–4–2 *Lion* stands buffer-to-buffer with MR 0–6–0 No.2537. Built by Sharp Stewart in 1867 as MR No.615, the class 1F 0–6–0 was renumbered 2357 in 1907 and survived in LMS ownership until withdrawal in December 1932. *Lion* had a varied career prior to restoration at Crewe Works in 1929, after which she had a new lease of life. She hauled the reproduction train during the 1930 celebrations and was exhibited afterwards at Liverpool Lime Street station. The locomotive's film career began in 1937 when it appeared in 'Victoria the Great', after which the locomotive was required for the London & Birmingham Railway centenary events of 1938. Following a period in store, *Lion* was used in the 1951 film 'The Lady with the Lamp', and the engine was in front of the cameras again for 'The Titfield Thunderbolt' of 1952.

Right: A naming ceremony with a difference. In this picture, taken on December 10 1935, we see Lord Stamp and Master Pat Rutherford, grandson of Lord Rutherford, the celebrated scientist, together with 'Jubilee' 4–6–0 No.5665 which the young man had just named *Lord Rutherford of Nelson*. Built in 1935, No.5665 ran for a short time before being named by Master Rutherford, who was presented with a model of the locomotive by Lord Stamp. The choice of name for the locomotive was most appropriate, since the locomotive was about to haul a train carrying a group of famous scientists to the opening of the new LMS Research Laboratory, at Derby.

Below: In September 1938 the LMS celebrated the centenary of the London & Birmingham Railway with a seven-day exhibition at Euston and here we see Coun. E.R. Canning JP., Lord Mayor of Birmingham, being sheltered from pouring rain at Euston whilst speaking at the opening of the exhibition. Also being sheltered under an umbrella is Lord Stamp, the LMS Chairman. Holding the 'brolly' is the Mayor of St Pancras.

NATIONALISATION

AFTER a quarter of a century of independent existence, the London Midland & Scottish Railway Company became part of the new British Railways organisation on January 1 1948. This last chapter looks at the arrival of the era of the state railway, as seen by the press photographers of the period. The LMS disappeared with Nationalisation, but the appointment of LMS-trained men like Robert Riddles, Roland Bond and E. S. Cox to senior engineering positions with British Railways meant that the future locomotive policy would show strong LMS trends: it was legacy which served BR well.

Top, left: The scene at Euston station in the closing minutes of December 31 1947, shortly before the departure of the final LMS train. Driver A. Grant (left) of Crewe and his fireman — whose name was regrettably not recorded — discuss train weight and other details with guard S.Smith, of Willesden. The locomotive was 'Patriot' 4—6—0 No.5508, seen here in 1946 livery.

Top, right: Farewell to the LMS: Guard Smith gives the 'rightaway' to the final LMS train from Euston, December 31 1947.

Left: On May 25 1948, painters obliterate the LMS lettering on a tender side: the British Railways era was under way.

Right: The early years of the new BR regime witnessed some interesting experimentation with liveries, in an attempt to produce the most attractive and practical colour scheme for the locomotive fleet. In this picture, Stanier 'Jubilee' 4–6–0 No.45565 *Victoria* is in green livery, with red, cream and grey lining, with the British Railways wording in full on the tender sides. The final choice for express passenger locomotives was Brunswick green, with orange and black lining.

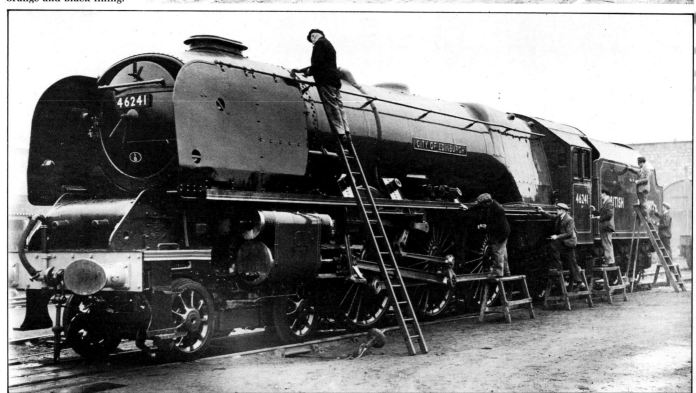

THE early livery experiments produced some unusual results, and Stanier 'Princess Coronation' 4–6–2 No.46241 *City of Edinburgh* is shorn of its streamlined cladding plates but retaining the distinctive sloping smokebox top, is painted in blue, with red, cream and grey lining. Happily, in their final years, 20 'Princess Coronation Pacifics' were repainted in crimson lake livery, albeit with BR insignia and markings, so to all intents and purposes the London Midland & Scottish Railway Company's primary passenger locomotive livery was retained into almost the final years of main line steam traction in Great Britain. This locomotive survived in traffic until September 1964, after which it was stored until December at Edge Hill shed, Liverpool prior to scrapping by Cashmore, of Great Bridge. Disposal of the 'Pacific' was complete by February 1965.